YORKSHIRE DIALECT CLASSICS

To all who love the sound of real dialect, especially
fellow-members of the Yorkshire Dialect Society,
the oldest society of its kind in the world.
Also dedicate to our fifteen grandchildren,
all of whom speak a somewhat different language.

Yorkshire Dialect Classics

compiled and edited by

Arnold Kellett

Dalesman

First published in 2005 by Dalesman
an imprint of
Country Publications Ltd
The Water Mill
Broughton Hall
Skipton
North Yorkshire
BD23 3AG

First edition 2005

ISBN 1 85568 226 5

Repro by PPS Grasmere, Leeds
Printed by Compass Press Ltd

Contents

Acknowledgements

I am most grateful to the Yorkshire Dialect Society for permission to reproduce material from its various publications, in particular, *Transactions* and the *Summer Bulletin*. The East Riding Dialect Society has also kindly allowed me to use its publication of the work of Arthur Jarratt.

Thanks are due to *Dalesman* magazine for permission to use items from my series 'Yorkshire Speyks', to the *Bradford Telegraph & Argus*, R Ackrill Ltd and to EMI Publications for the monologue by R P Weston and Bert Lee. Apologies are offered if any copyright permission has been missed.

A number of items have previously appeared in *The White Rose Garland* (1949) and my own *Basic Broad Yorkshire* (1992), as well as the anthology I co-edited with Ian Dewhirst, *A Century of Yorkshire Dialect* (1997). As these three books are now out of print, it seemed sensible to give selected pieces from them a new lease of life.

Thanks are also due to the following for permission to reproduce illustrations:

Margaret Clarkson, front cover, pp34, 37, 43, 47, 99, 106, 115, 119; Peter Kearney, pp17, 30, 33, 39, 51, 55, 58, 63, 94, 98, 103, 111, 114, 122, 126; Pete Lindup, p23.

Helpful individuals I especially wish to thank are Muriel Shackleton, former editor of *Summer Bulletin*, Brian Spencer, editor of *Transactions*, Michael Park, secretary of the Yorkshire Dialect Society, David W Rank of the East Riding Dialect Society, Barbara Marcroft, Ruth Ward — and Mark Whitley of Country Publications Ltd. It goes without saying that I continue to be indebted to Pat, my wife, for invaluable, irreplaceable support of a lass from 't' right side o' t' Pennines'.

Arnold Kellett

What is Yorkshire dialect?

In the 1920s, when most working-class people tended to speak dialect, a doctor in the Keighley area wrote an account for the Yorkshire Dialect Society of some of his experiences with his patients. He described how on one occasion he went to the home of an old farmer who was very seriously ill and thought to be dying. He examined him, and having found no perceptible pulse he turned to the wife and said: 'I'm sorry love. But I'm afraid poor John has passed away'.

'Nay, doctor', came a feeble voice from the man in the bed. 'Ah ammot dee-ad yet!'

'Thee 'od thi tongue, lad', snapped his wife. 'T' doctor knaws better ner thee!'

This true story serves to illustrate an important point about Yorkshire dialect. In recent years it has largely disappeared from everyday life, and real dialect speakers are now an endangered species. But, like the old chap in this story, dialect is not dead yet.

True, it is not in a healthy state, and everywhere it is being replaced by what we in the Dialect Society call 'local speech', which retains the accent and intonation of earlier days, but hardly any of the vocabulary and idiom which makes real dialect so distinctive. Somebody from London, for example, might assume that Yorkshire people who speak with a strong accent (we keep our vowels open in Yorkshire!) are 'talking dialect'. But it is nothing of the kind. If they were to speak the traditional dialect — the everyday speech of earlier generations — 'off-comed-uns' would hardly be able to understand a word of it.

Does this mean, then, that real dialect, if not yet actually extinct, will eventually become what we call a dead language? I'm afraid it will. The continuing evolution of colloquial language makes this inevitable. And I do not share the view that dialects do not die, but only change. When the change reaches such a point that the local speech scarcely resembles its earlier form, we must accept that a demise has taken place. It is no use saying that Italian, French and Spanish, for example, are simply changed forms of Latin. They have their own identity, and look back on Latin as a deceased, though honourable, parent — a dead language, in the sense that it is no longer spoken.

Yet all is not lost. We do not disregard Latin, Greek, Sanskrit and so forth, just because nobody still speaks such languages. Nor do we neglect Chaucer just because nobody speaks Middle English any more. In the case of Yorkshire dialect, we are in a happier position. A minority still speak it, and even more still understand it and remember it with affection.

So we have an opportunity we must not miss. While Yorkshire dialect is still known and loved — and is at least within living memory — we should do our best to pin it down, while we still have time. That is the motivation for my own years of talks and books on our dialect. I am, I suppose, a linguistic conservationist. Parallel with our commendable effort to conserve buildings, beauty spots and archaeological items, I believe we need to research and display the artefacts of the language we call dialect.

In a sense this book constitutes a kind of literary museum, with its specimens set out in roughly chronological order. But it is much more than that. These specimens can be brought to life again — either through personal reading, or through being read aloud by one of our surviving dialect-speakers. To hear dialect read competently and enthusiastically can be a delightful experience.

Before we go any further, though, we should clear up two possible misapprehensions, often found amongst those who are not familiar with Yorkshire dialect.

The first is the idea that dialect is a quaint and comical kind of speech — and a corruption of normal English. This may be true of what sometimes is mistaken for dialect — a slovenly, lazy way of talking, full of bad grammar and slang — much of this of recent origin. True dialect, far from being a deviation from the official standard, is essentially an earlier form of English, a language in its own right, as we shall see in the following chapter briefly outlining its origins. Although it is closely associated with humour — as many of these items will show — the actual dialect, blunt and vivid though it may be, is not funny in itself, nor are Yorkshire dialect speakers necessarily stand-up comedians.

The second fallacious idea is that dialect is just a matter of curious words and phrases. This is an impression unintentionally given by the BBC project *Voices* (2005), which — no doubt inevitably — gave a great deal of attention to different words used for the same thing in different parts of the country, along with interesting local terms and expressions. What we must not overlook is that dialect, particularly in Yorkshire, has produced a considerable body of literature — poetry and prose written entirely in dialect, not merely conversational snatches of it used in novels or plays.

We have, in fact, a whole repository of printed dialect material, most of it from an age when 'broad Yorkshire' was a living language. Much of it is light and ephemeral, some of it of real literary merit — but all of it is of linguistic and sociological interest. It is undeniably part of our culture, and because there is, I am convinced, more dialect material to be found in Yorkshire than in any other county, it really deserves to be collected and presented in the form of a book like this.

This is not to say that I regard this as a definitive anthology. I have agonised over which items should be included, very much aware of some I reluctantly had to leave out because space is obviously limited in a book designed to stimulate interest rather than give an exhaustive coverage. I have, however, tried to make a representative selection, and to strike a balance between the serious and humorous, between town and country — and between the two major divisions of West Riding dialect on the one hand, and North and East Riding dialect on the other. Above all, I have made a point of giving the original, authentic form of this material — not the half-remembered, misquoted versions sometimes passed off as genuine.

Readers who are not used to Yorkshire dialect (and perhaps even some who are) may not at first find all this easy reading. But be patient. You will soon get accustomed to it, and the glossary at the back will help you with the words you may not know.

The contents of this book are, of course, a world away from what most people read today, when fiction and fantasy predominate. But real life can be at least as entertaining, especially if we are enabled to glimpse the realities of days gone by, when life was harsh and restricted, yet paradoxically touched with joy.

Moreoever, in an age of electronic globalisation, when everything is becoming monotonously the same, it is good to assert the distinctive characteristics of our various regions and counties, and a refreshing change to experience what I believe to be the specially piquant and heart-warming flavour of the three ancient Ridings of Yorkshire.

A brief history of
Yorkshire dialect

Yorkshire dialect has its roots — like the English language as a whole — in the speech of the Germanic tribes who invaded and settled in our land in the fifth century. It is often incorrectly stated that our ancestors here in Yorkshire were called Saxons. But these settled in the south — in Essex ('the land of the East Saxons'), Sussex (the South Saxons) and so on.

In the Midlands, East Anglia and the North were the more numerous Angles — according to St Bede, so called because they came from the angle of land we now call Schleswig-Holstein. It was these ancestors of ours after whom England is named, literally meaning 'the land of the Angles'.

We describe the speech of pre-Norman England as Old English or Anglo-Saxon, but there was a difference between the way the Angles and Saxons spoke (the origin of the north/south difference today) and also a difference within the vast territory occupied by the Angles. The speech of their kingdom of Mercia, which covered the Midlands, gradually spread into Yorkshire and formed the basis of West Riding dialect, spoken approximately from the valley of the Wharfe southwards. The speech of the kingdom of Northumbria (all the land north of the Humber) formed the basis of the North Riding and East Riding dialects, which are similar to each other. Following the custom of the Yorkshire Dialect society, these are abbreviated as WR, and NR and ER (and sometimes NER when the dialect could be from either area).

As will be obvious from the items in this book, there is a considerable difference between WR and NER dialects. In general the speech of the West Riding is louder and more incisive, perhaps reflecting life in the mills, mines and steelworks,

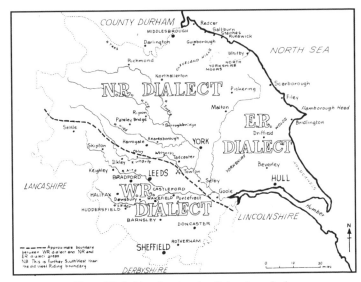

Map of Yorkshire showing the dialect boundaries.

when people had to shout to make themselves heard above the industrial noise. The speech of the North and East Ridings seems to be quiet and gentle in comparison, reflecting life in the countryside. There are also some differences in vocabulary. For example, a friend of mine, when a child, had a grandma in the West Riding who gave her *spice*. When she visited her other grandma in the East Riding she received *goodies* — both words meaning 'sweets'. There are also differences of style. In WR the familiar form 'thou' is *tha* (or *ta*), in NER *thoo*. In WR 'I am' is *Ah'm* or *Aw'm*; in NER it is *Ah's*. The biggest difference, however, is in vowel sounds, as illustrated by the following, which serve as a pattern:

WR	NER	
dahn	*doon*	down
schooil	*skeeal*	school
dooant	*deeant*	don't
speyk	*speeak*	speak
coit	*cooat*	coat

However, the two main branches of Yorkshire dialect do have much in common, and both are rich in Anglo-Saxon sounds. For example, words like *lang* (long) and *finnd* (find) preserve the vowels we still find in modern German. Many Anglo-Saxon words which have disappeared from Standard English, or changed their meaning, can still be heard in Yorkshire dialect. To be *starved* is not to be very hungry, but to be very cold (from Anglo-Saxon *steorfan*, 'to suffer intensely'). Shoppers who say *'Nay, Ah can't thoil t' brass'* don't mean they can't afford the money, but that they don't think they can justify spending the money on that particular item — and this shade of meaning in *thoil* (Anglo-Saxon *tholian*, 'to bear, endure') has been lost from Standard English. Even when Yorkshire folk used to say *'Ah axed 'im'* (I asked him) they were not ignorantly putting the 'k' before the 's', but unconsciously preserving the Anglo-Saxon verb *acsian* (to ask).

The next stage of development was brought about by the invasion of the Vikings in the ninth century — the Danes settling in the flatter area around York and dividing the county into three Ridings, a word derived from the Scandinavian *thrithjungr* (a third). The Norwegians, or Norsemen, came from their settlement in Ireland and settled in the Dales — in Swaledale, for example, where we find their words in places like Keld, Muker and Gunnerside (Gunnar was a hero in their sagas).

Viking words are found all over Yorkshire, in place-names ending with -by, -thorpe and -thwaite, for example, and in common words in our dialect, such as *addle* (to earn), *lig* (to lie), *laik* (to play), *stee* (ladder), *teem* (to pour), *tyke* (dog), *ey up!* (look out!) etc. You may notice that sometimes the dialect used for 'child' is *bairn*. This is the Anglo-Saxon word *bearn*. At other times it may be *barn*. This is the Viking form of the word.

The final stage of the evolution of English followed William the Conqueror's invasion of 1066. These French-speaking Normans (originally Norsemen who had settled in northern France) imposed their authority on the whole country, and French was spoken to such an extent that it attached itself to the existing mixture of Anglo-Saxon and Viking, forming about a third of what we call Middle English, the language in which Chaucer wrote in the late fourteenth century. A few French terms survived in Yorkshire dialect which are unknown in Standard English. My own favourite is *buffit* (a low stool), which was the original meaning of *buffet* in Norman French.

For a while there was no standard form of English, only the varieties found in different parts of the country. But from 1476 Caxton's printing press began to disseminate the kind of English spoken and written by educated Londoners. It was also spread by people like government officials and merchants travelling from London into all parts of the country.

Soon the local dialects were being regarded as an inferior form of speech — ironically so, because what became known as Standard English, along with Received Pronunciation, had itself started out as a mere dialect — that of the London area. Now it was busy supplanting all the other dialects, and a distinction was increasingly being made between 'official' English and the speech of industrial workers, labourers, servants, fishermen, farmers and country-people.

The great enemy of dialect (which from the linguistic point-of-view was just as good as Standard English, and in some ways more subtle) was education. Once children had been taught to read and write they were expected to talk like all the others who could read and write. Indeed, most of the words they used in everyday dialect — words like *summat* and *nowt*, for example — they would be unlikely to find in print at all. As early as the 1850s we can see in reports of school inspectors that there was a deliberate policy of discouraging all dialect and strong local accent.

Unknown in schools, there had been a few isolated attempts to put dialect into print — John Ray's *Collection of Northern Words* (1674), George Martin's *A Yorkshire Dialogue* (1683) and the first printed version by John Aubrey of *The Lyke Wake Dirge* (1686). In the early nineteenth century, influenced by Robert Burns, the first real Yorkshire dialect poetry was published, written by a self-educated farmer, David Lewis. But it was the emergence of the dialect almanacks — the first published by Abel Bywater in Sheffield in 1830 — which gave vernacular speech a real shot in the arm. For the first time ordinary people could see their native speech in print, take a pride in it, have fun with it and keep it alive. No fewer than eighteen different dialect almanacks were published in the West Riding alone — all at easily affordable prices. Though the humour in them has dated considerably, they provide us with plenty of evidence about the daily life and outlook of dialect-speaking communities.

Academics were now taking an interest in dialect. The most important of these was Joseph Wright (1855-1930). At the age of six he started work as a donkey-boy in a quarry at Windhill, Shipley, and then moved to Salt's Mill. Illiterate until he was fifteen, he then started on a remarkable programme of self-education, eventually specialising in languages and becoming Professor of Comparative Philology at Oxford. He never lost touch with his Yorkshire roots, and in 1892 published his *Grammar of the Dialect of Windhill*, which his university colleagues at first thought was a joke — until they realised that Professor Wright was treating Yorkshire dialect as a subject worthy of serious study. 'Ahr Jooa', as he was affectionately known, finally published his monumental six-volume *English Dialect Dictionary* in 1905.

This famous dictionary was based on collections of words and phrases made by committees all over the country. The one in Bradford, having finished its work for Professor Wright in 1897, decided not to disband, but to continue to encourage interest in dialect by founding the Yorkshire Dialect Society, now the oldest in the world. This society has for more than a century arranged meetings all over the county, at which members can read poems and stories, often their own work. It has also published a considerable amount of dialect material, and still issues the respected academic journal *Transactions* and the creative dialect writing of the *Summer Bulletin*. One of its editors, Professor F W Moorman, was the first to make a collection of dialect poems, published in 1916.

Dialect continues to be heard at various other meetings in Yorkshire, such as those of the University of the Third Age, and the East Riding Dialect Society, with its own publications, founded in 1984. Apart from such meetings, there is little public utterance of Yorkshire dialect, and gone are the days of popular recitations by John Hartley and Ben Preston, plays by such writers as J R Gregson, the dialect patter of such comedians as Tom Foy and Albert Modley, and, later, Charlie Williams. Nor do we have such radio and television personalities as Wilfred Pickles (1907-1978) to popularise West Riding speech. Similarly, the old almanacks, followed by dialect writers in the papers, such as 'Buxom Betty' in *the Bradford Telegraph and Argus*, have all disappeared. However, the writing and performance of dialect still has an outlet through some of the festivals, notably the Mrs Sunderland Competition (founded in 1889) in Huddersfield Town Hall.

What of the state and status of dialect today? The war of attrition against dialect, and the pressure to conform to a standard, has continued. The real anti-dialect influence nowadays is the non-stop flow of language from radio and television — not so much Standard English and Received Pronunciation as estuary English, with its un-Yorkshire style, often full of slick clichés and predictable, conventional phrases.

It is true that television soap operas include plenty of northern speech, including that of Yorkshire. There is hardly ever any actual dialect, but, at least, northern vowels and intonation are being heard more and more. To speak educated English with a Yorkshire accent is becoming generally acceptable. To speak real dialect, however, is likely to be responded to with amused tolerance, as something ignorant and incomprehensible.

There is no doubt that dialect has suffered increasingly rapid erosion — through the pressure of the media, through fundamental changes in everyday life, especially a new social mobility, and the disappearance of traditional communities dependent on mills and mines, on farming and fishing. Yet although dialect is now in serious, even terminal, decline, interest in it seems to be experiencing a revival.

It is as though we have at last realised that Yorkshire dialect really is an important and intriguing part of our heritage — a point this anthology seeks to demonstrate.

Pronunciation and spelling

It is not easy to read Yorkshire dialect, not if we want an idea of how it sounds. Yet it is almost always spelt phonetically. The trouble is that there is no agreed way of spelling it, so we have to get used to the style and idiosyncrasies of each individual writer.

In the following chapters I have mostly kept the original form, but here and there simplified it and rationalised it in order to make it easier for the reader. In particular, I have altered those spellings I regard as ridiculous — included, I assume, to make the dialect look as quaint as possible. What on earth is the point of writing *sed* for 'said', or *tawk* for 'talk', and so forth, when the sound is the same as in Standard English? In case of words like *laff* (laugh) it is justified, because the writer is making sure we pronounce it with a short 'a'. The same applies to *luv* (love), a spelling intended to emphasise the short, northern vowel. But I really see no need to produce odd-looking words like *oop* (up) and *coom* (come), when we all know that here dialect uses a 'u', as in 'book' rather than 'touch'.

The only scientific way to put these dialect sounds into print is to use the IPA (International Phonetic Alphabet), a system of letters and symbols indicating a particular consonant or vowel. Once you have learnt these you can record and read back the dialect exactly as it sounds. The trouble is that the IPA — as in the system used by Joseph Wright in his book on the dialect of Windhill — looks like a mass of hieroglyphics, and is more off-putting than the printed dialect.

The real way to learn how the dialect sounds is to listen to it being read by dialect-speakers — from the appropriate area. It is not ideal, for example, to hear a John Hartley poem in West Riding dialect read by a speaker from the North and East Ridings, or to hear *Goodies* read by somebody from the

West Riding. Listening to recordings and tapes can, of course, be a practical way of getting used to the way it should sound.

Here are a few points which we need to bear in mind when reading Yorkshire dialect.

Yorkshire vowels are pure vowels

The term 'broad Yorkshire' (originally referring to its size, the biggest county in England) carries with it the idea of a speech that is rather crude and rough. Yet the vowels used in Yorkshire and in other northern counties are virtually the same as heard in French, German, Italian and Spanish — and, indeed, most of the world's languages. Whereas the Received Pronunciation of Standard English has rounded vowels like 'ay-ee', 'aye-ee and 'o-oo', the equivalent dialect vowel may just be a single sound. For example, a word like *go* in dialect is not rounded to 'go-oo', except in parts south of Leeds, where it has a short 'o' (as in 'got') plus an 'oo'.

Yorkshire double vowels

Having said that dialect vowels are not rounded as in Standard English, it must be noted that double vowels, rather like diphthongs, are very common. For example, in West Riding speech we have words like *dooar* (door) and *'eead* (head) written like this, but pronounced 'doo-ar' and 'ee-ad'. In East Riding the equivalent is *deear*, pronounced 'dee-ar'.

A similar double vowel occurs in North and East Riding in words like *naam* (name) pronounced 'nay-em'. Curiously, the same vowel is heard in the Huddersfield and Holmfirth areas. Here the normal West Riding sound in *dahn* (down), for example, sounds like 'day-en', and is usually written as *daan, deean* or *deyan*.

Older West Riding speech had a double vowel in words like *sooin* (soon), pronounced 'soo-in', and an attractive intrusive 'ee' in words like *meeusic*, pronounced 'mee-oo-sic'. A similar sound is heard in North Riding words like 'book', written as *beuk* or *bewk*.

The dipthong in *owt, nowt* and *browt* in most parts of Yorkshire is not the 'ow' sound in Standard English 'now', but more like 'aw-oo'.

Short vowels

We have already noted the vowel in *luv*. All the 'u' sounds in Yorkshire dialect are like this, with no distinction between the vowels in words like 'cut' and 'put'.

The 'a' sound, as in *brass* (money), is always short, including words where there might be a longer vowel in Received Pronunciation such as 'bath' or 'grass'. If the longer 'a' sound is used it is usually written as in *dahn* (down) or *wahr* (worse) and *wahrm* (warm), the latter rhyming with 'harm'.

The 'i' sound is usually short, as in *bit*, but when it is a longer standard diphthong, as in 'time', a rather flatter dialect vowel may be shown as *tahme*.

The vowel in words like 'first' tends to be short in dialect, so this might be written as *fust* or *fost*.

Short vowels are always pronounced if there is a double consonant, eg *ovver*, *finnd* and *watter*.

Consonants

These are sharp and clear in Yorkshire dialect — except for two which we dispense with altogether.

First, there is a systematic dropping of 'h' (as in French), which is usually replaced by an apostrophe. Even if it appears in print it is not sounded — except for emphasis in a mild curse, such as *Oh, hummer!*

Secondly, there is a systematic dropping of the final 'g' in '-ing', as in *laikin'* (playing) etc. The 'ing' sound does not have the 'g' pronounced as in normal English 'finger' (fing-ger) — making it like 'singer'.

Note that in NER the 'r' is always pronounced, including words such as *nivver*, *worrker* and *orr* (her). There is also a softening of the 't' and 'd' in words like *dhroondid* (drowned) and *throosies* (trousers).

The glottal stop

This is natural to a speaker of Yorkshire dialect, but very difficult for Standard English speakers to imitate. I once had the greatest difficulty, during the production of a radio play, in getting a London actor, taking the part of a Yorkshireman, to pronounce phrases like *in t' cave*. He persisted in saying 'in cave'. Then he tried to get the effect of the glottal stop by counting a second or two between the words — 'in...cave'. This was even worse, so we settled for 'int cave', which tended to sound like 'inter cave'. In reality the 't' is not actually sounded, but is replaced by a brisk opening and shutting of the glottis at the top of the windpipe.

In parts of the East Riding, incidentally, they don't even bother with a glottal stop but omit the article altogether in phrases like *on teeable* (on the table).

Favourite Yorkshire
dialect sayings

A full explanation of these and other popular sayings can be found in the compiler's *Yorkshire Dictionary of Dialect, Tradition and Folklore* and *Basic Broad Yorkshire*, which also sets out the grammar of Yorkshire dialect.

A canny attitude to other folk

Ther's nowt so queer as fowk... Ther' all on 'em queer, bar thee an' me — an' sometimes Ah'm nut so sewer abaht thee! (WR)

The Yorkshire motto

(Said tongue in cheek)
'Ear all, see all, say nowt;
Eyt all, sup all, pay nowt;
An' if ivver tha does owt fer nowt —
Do it fer thissen! (WR)

A North Riding motto

Wi mense tak what's yer awn;
Wi pluck 'od whats yer awn,
An' mak that fet;
Gi 'e wi oppen 'and —
But nivver let friendship spoil a bargin.

The Yorkshireman's coat of arms

(Dialect verse explaining the coat of arms first drawn by Thomas Tegg of London in 1812, poking fun at Yorkshire people, who are symbolised by a flea, a fly, a magpie and a hanging flitch of bacon)

A flea, a fly, a magpie an' a bacon flitch
Is t' Yorksherman's coit of arms;
An' t' reason they've chozzen theease things sooa rich,
Is 'cos they hev all special charms;
A flea will bite 'ooivver it can —
An' sooa, mi lads, will a Yorksherman!
A fly 'll sup wi Dick, Tom or Dan —
An' sooa, bi Gow, will a Yorksherman!
A magpie can talk fer a terrible span —
An' sooa an' all can a Yorksherman!
A flitch is nooa good while it's hung, yer'll agree —
An' nooa mooare is a Yorksherman, dooan't yer see? (WR)

A Yorkshire toast

'Ere's tiv us — all on us — an me an all!
May wi nivver want nowt, nooan on us —
Ner me nawther!(WR)

An East Riding version of this toast goes:
'Ere's tiv us — all on us,
All on us ivver;
May neean on us want nowt,
Neean on us nivver.

There is also the West Riding variation:
'Ere's ter me,
An' mi wife's 'usband —
Nooan forgettin' missen.

A Yorkshire grace

Before a meal there is the traditional grace:
God bless us all, an' mak us able
Ta eyt all t' stuff 'at's on this table.

To follow an ungenerous meal there is the satirical verse:
We thank the Lord for what wi've getten:
Bud if mooare 'ad been cutten
Ther'd mooare 'a' been etten. (WR)

The Yorkshire coat of arms.

Saying before a meal, said to encourage diners to fill up with Yorkshire pudding — a first course, with onion gravy — so they would have less appetite for the meat, which was more expensive

Them 'at eyts mooast puddin' gets mooast meyt. (WR)

Self-deprecating sayings
Shak' a bridle ovver a Yorksherman's grave — an' 'e'll gerr up an' steal t' oss.

Yorkshire born an' Yorkshire bred,
Strong in t' arm an' thick in t' 'ead.

Tha can allus tell a Yorkshireman — but not much!

Obsolete forms of counting sheep
(Numbers probably going back to Celtic times. This sample is from Wensleydale.)
1. Yan   2. Tean   3. Tither   4. Mither   5. Pip   6. Teazer
7. Leazer   8. Catra   9. Horna   10. Dick   11. Yan-dick

12. Tean-dick   13. Tither-dick   14.Mither-dick 15. Bumper
16. Yan-a-bum   17. Tean-a-bum   18. Tither-a-bum
19. Mither-a-bum   20. Jigger

Sayings concerning health
(In descending order of well-being)
Champion!
Nicely
Nobbut middlin'
Nobbut varry middlin'
Just fair
Nobbut dowly
Badly
Failin'
Goin' dahn t' nick

'E leeaks a bad leeak (NER)

'E looks a reight poor object (WR)

Tha's on t' mend … Tha'll clog ageean … Tha'll nooan pop thi clogs just yet! (WR)

Sayings concerning places
Wibsa' (Wibsey) and Pudsa (Pudsey) … wheere t' ducks fly back'ards rooad ter keep t' muck aht o' the'r een.

Wibsa and Pudsa gawbies (simpletons)

Pudsa, wheeare the've all bald 'eeads, 'cos the' pull 'em aht o' t' pit wi suckers … an' wheeare the've treeacle mines.

Marsden, wheeare the' put t' pigs in t' wall ter listen ter t' band.

Ossett, wheeare the' black-leead t' tram-lines.

Slowit (Slaithwaite), wheeare the' raked mooin aht o' t' cut.

T' Wharfe is clear, an' t' Aire is lythe;
Where t' Aire drahns one, t' Wharfe drahns five.

Castleford lasses may weel bi fair,
For the' wesh in t' Calder an' sind in t' Aire.

Yattoners (of Great Ayton) wade ower t' beck ti seeave t' brig.

Runs'ick (Runswick) men wiv all the'r toil
Comes ti Steeas (Staithes) ti sell the'r oil.
Steeas men wiv all the'r nuts
Gans ti Runs'ick ter fill the'r guts.

Steeas yackers (acres), flither-pickers (limpet gatherers),
'errin' guts for garters

Barrowby Hills an' Newton Broos
Them is t' spots fer 'osses an' coos.

Sutton boiled mutton,
Brotherton beef;
Ferrybridge bonny lasses,
Knottingley thief.

As sure as a lahse i' Pomfret (Pontefract).

Cahr quite — same as the' do i' Birstall.

E's a Leeds loiner.

T' Linthwaite leeadboilers

T' terrible knitters o' Dent

Gowcar (Golcar) — wheeare t' lilies comes thru.

Begin ageean — like t' Meltham singers

Let's say it all ower ageean like t' clerk o' Beeston

Boroughbridge keep oot o' t' way,
For Auldboro' toon
Ah'll ding doon!
(Said by the Devil before throwing the three Devil's Arrows)

When Roseberry Topping wears a cap,
Let Cleveland then beware a clap

Bedale bonnets an' Bedale faces
Finnd nowt ti beat 'em
I' onny places.

From Hell, Hull an' Halifax
Good Lord deliver us!

Halifax is built o' wax,
Heptonstall o' stooane;
I' Halifax ther's bonny lasses,
I' Heptonstall ther's nooan.

Keighley kay-legged uns.
(When rickets was common)

A Scarborough warning.
(A punch first, then a warning or explanation)

Thoo'll knaw which is t' bull
Bi t' ring in 'is snoot:
Seea deean't stand an' gawp —
It's taame ti git oot!
(Farmer's notice on a gate at Duck Bridge, near Danby)

Saying concerning the use of the familiar form
(ie thee/thoo, tha/ta, thy/thi, thine)
Ey! Dooan't thee thee-tha me! Tha thee-tha's them 'at thee-
tha's thee.

In Sheffield the 'th' can be 'd', so there is the greeting: 'Nah
den dee!'

Sayings concerning individuals
Tha's marrer ter Bonny! (You're just like Napoleon!)

As black as t' Divil's nuttin' bag.

A whistlin' woman an' a crowin' 'en
Brings t' Owd Lad aht of 'is den.

As throng as Throp's wife ('oo brewed, weshed an baked on t'
same day, then 'enged ersen wi t' dish claht).

As idle as Ludlam's dog 'at laid itsen dahn ter bark
(*or* 'at leaned it' 'eead agen t' wall ter bark).

'E wor stood theeare like Jooa Locke.
(Statue of the Barnsley benefactor).

As queer as Dick's 'at-band, 'at went nine times rahnd — an'
still wouldn't tee.

Insults

blether-'eead, claht-'eead, wazzock, gurt gawmless gawp-'eead
daft awporth
slack set-up
same as a man made o' band
tha frames wahr ner a cat i' pattens
'e's shakked i' bits
tha's wahr ner mi ant Kate
a reight nip-screw
that mean 'e 'd nip a curn i' two (WR)
'e'd skin a lop fer t' hide an' tallow (NER)
'e's bow-legged wi' brass
'e couldn't stop a pig in a ginnel
'e's double-fisted an' threpple-throited
'e's as leet-gi'en as a posser-'eead.

Describing places in a mess

What a hoile! (WR)
A bonny hubbleshoo! (NR)
An 'oose lahke Fondbridge Fair (ER)

Terms for left-handed

Cack-'anded, gallock-'anded, gawky-'anded, kaggy-'anded,
golly-'anded, dawky-'anded, dolly-posh, cuddy-wifted etc.

A multi-purpose WR phrase

1 *Nah then?* (Hello! How are things?)
2 *Nah then!* (Here we are etc)
3 *Na then, lad?!* (All right etc)
4 *Na then!* (Watch it! That's enough!)

West Riding 'oiles

Most people seem to know *'Put t' wood in t' 'oile!'* (Shut the door!), which probably originated in the mines, when children as *trappers* opened and shut the square holes of ventilation shafts. Here the word means 'hole', but is also commonly used for 'place', as in these typical examples:

Bobby-'oile (police station), *cake-'oile* (mouth), *chip-'oile* (fish and chip shop), *coil-'oile* (coal-cellar), *delph-'oile* (quarry), *jerry-'oile* (low pub), *kall-'oile* (place for gossip), *lug-'oile* (ear-hole), *mengle-'oile* (wash-house), *muck-'oile* (dirty, messy place), *nooase-'oile* (nostril), *penny-'oile* (mill gate-house), *pey-'oile* (pea and pie shop), *pig-'oile* (stye), *smoot-'oile* (hole in a wall or hedge for sheep), *stee-'oile* (stile), *tuffil-'oile* (garden shed) ... and many more.

Similes

As common as muck
As black as t' fire-back
As daft as a brush
As gawmless as a gooise nicked i' t' 'eead
As sackless as a booat-'oss
As deeaf as a yat-stowp
As blinnd as a mowdiwarp
As cheerful as a chapel-lowsin'
As tough as wengby
As snod as glass
As whist as a mahse
As kittle as a moos-thrap
As leet as a cleg
As fahl as a ripped clog
As dry as a lime-burner's clog
As drunk as a fuzzock
As druffen as a wheel-'eead
As mawngy as an owd cat
As fit as a butcher's dog
As creeaked as a dog's hind leg
As pleeased as a pissimer
As brant as a 'oose-sahde
As bald as a blether o' lard
As fat as a mawk
As white as a privy mawk
As thin as a lat
As streight as a yard o' pump watter

Old Amos

A character who has appeared in the *Dalesman* since 1953, created by Rowland Lindup. Here are just a few of his observations.

Owd Amos, who has been dispensing his pithy comments for over fifty years.

Fowk are like tea. Tha can nivver judge o' the'r quality till the' get into 'ot watter.

When bairns are quiet it doesn't allus mean the'r planning' mischief. They may 'ave done it already.

Nay, lad. Ah'm not t'owdest inhabitant. He died years ago.

Has-ta ivver noticed 'at t' brass tha owes is allus mooare than tha reckoned — an' t' brass owed ter thee is allus less than tha thowt?

Nivver tell a chap 'is faults. Tell 'em to 'is wife instead. Shoo'll be reight suited — an' 'e'll get to 'ear abaht 'em just t' same.

Tha mun mak t' mooast o' thissen. It's all tha's getten!

T' 'ardest work of all is doin' nowt.

Well, Ah dooan't knaw 'ow old you are — but you certainly dooan't look it.

Aye, lad. Ah'm ninety-nine terday. One mooare year, an' Ah s'll be a centipede.

Proverbs and other sayings

By no means an exhaustive list, but a few samples of Yorkshire wit and wisdom.

Wheeare ther's muck, ther's brass
There's nowt good that's cheap
Strength goes in at t' mahth

Etten jock's sooin forgotten
T' third generation goes back ter t' clogs.
Nivver judge a blade bi t' heft
Ah'm that 'ungry mi belly thinks mi throit's cut
It's nut jannock
Ah'm fair capped! It caps owt!

(From the days when the shilling (5p) coin was a *bob*)
Ahr Bob says 'at if your Bob
Doesn't pay ahr Bob
That theeare bob 'at your Bob
Owes ahr Bob ...
Ahr Bob's goin' to 'ev your Bob
Bobbed dahn in t' bobby-'oile!'

'E talks an' 'e says nowt
Sh' telled t' tale from t' thread ter t' needle
'E chuntered a bucketful
Nowt said needs no mendin'

(Hiding from the rent collector, especially in the Barnsley area)
'Ere dahn i' t' cellar-'oile,
Wheeare t' muck slahts on t' winders,
We've used all us coil up
An' we'r reight dahn ter t' cinders —
But if t' bum-baillie comes.
'E 'll nivver finnd us! WR

It's black ovver Bill's mother's
It's 'ossin' ter slaht
Well, Ah'll go ter t' fooit of ahr stairs!
Wi mun keep t' band in t' nick
Ah reckon nowt to it. Ah can't reckon it up
'As t' ivver 'ugged a pooak up a stee till thi rigg warked?
Come on, lad. Frame thissen!
Ah've an 'eead like a set pot
Ah wor fair starved, reight nithered
Een stuck aht like chapel 'at-pegs
Na, think on! Ther's nowt wrong wi reight fowk
Come thi ways in!

Dialect verse

These poems are approximately in chronological order, starting with a fragment from the first known Yorkshire poet, Caedmon, the cowherd who in about AD 600 became a lay-brother in Whitby Abbey, and was encouraged by Saint Hilda to write down the poems he composed. The few lines preserved by Saint Bede in his History of the English Church and People *are in the speech of the Angles of Northumbria (the part later called the North Riding) and, although this is Old English, it is the basis of the language which became Yorkshire dialect. So it seems fitting to give this as our first known piece of local poetry, with a translation.*

Caedmon's Hymn to Creation

Nu scylun hergan hefaenricaes ward,
Metudes maecti ond his modgidanc,
werc wuldurfadur, sue he wundra gihwaes,
eci dryctin, or astelide,
He aerist scop, aelda barnum
heben til hrofa, haleg scepen;
tha middungeard moncynnes ward,
eci dryctin, after tiade,
firum foldu, frea allmectig.

Now let us praise the Guardian of Heaven,
The majesty of his might and the thought of his mind,
The work of the Glory-father,
How he, worker of wonders,
The eternal Lord, beginning established;
He first shaped for earth's children
Heaven as a roof, the holy Creator;
Then the middle-earth mankind's Guardian,
The eternal Lord, afterwards adorned.

From the Second Shepherds' Play *in the Townley Cycle, written some time between 1400 and 1450, here is an extract in Middle English from the scene where three shepherds visit the stable in Bethlehem, paying their respects, and each presenting a little gift.*

The Wakefield Mystery Plays
(extract)

3rd Shepherd. He spake of a barne
In Bedlem, I you warne.
1st Shepherd. That betokens yond starne;
Let us seke him there
2nd Shepherd. To Bedlem he bad that we should gang;
I am full feeared that we tarry too lang.
3rd Shepherd. Be merry and not sad — of myrth is oure sang!
Everlastyng glad to mede may we fang,
Withoutt noyse.
1st Shepherd. Hy we theder forthy,
If we be wet and weary,
To that child and that lady;
We have it not to lose.

1st Shepherd. Hayll, comly and clene! Hayll, yong child!
Hayll, maker, as I meyne, of a madyn so mylde! ...
Lo, he merries,
Lo, he laughys, my swetyng!
A wel fare metyng!
I have holden my hetyng *(promise)* ...
Have a bob of cherries.

2nd Shepherd. Hayll, sufferan savyoure, for thou hast us sought!
Hayll, frely foyde *(noble child)* and flowre, that all thyng has wrought!
Hayll, full of favoure, that made all of nought!
Hayll! I kneyll and I cowre. A byrd have I brought
To my barne.

Hayll, lytyll tyne mop *(tiny moppet)*!
Of oure crede thou art crop *(head)*;
I would drynk on thy cop *(cup)*,
Lytyll day-starne.

3rd Shepherd. Hayll, derlyng dere, full of Godhede!
I pray thee be nere when that I have nede.
Hayll, swete is thy chere *(face)*! My hart would blede
To see thee sytt here in so poore weede,
With no pennies.
Hayll! Put furth thy dall *(hand)*!
I bring thee but a ball:
Have and play thee withal,
And go to the tennis...

1st Shepherd. Fare well, lady, so fare to beholde
With thy childe on thi knee.
2nd Shepherd. But he liggs full cold.
Lord, well is me! Now we go, thou behold.
3rd Shepherd. Forsothe, allredy it semys to be told
Full oft.
1st Shepherd. What grace we have fun!
2nd Shepherd. Com furth; now are we won!
3rd Shepherd. To syng are we bun —
(They go out singing)

Here is one of the very oldest of Yorkshire's dialect songs, especially associated with the Cleveland district of the northernmost part of the county. Although it did not appear in print until 1686, it had been sung for centuries at funerals, and concerns the ancient ritual of carrying the lyke *(corpse) on the traditional route over the moors to the burial place — a journey mirrored in the song by the progress of the* sawl *(soul) towards Purgatory — and, if good works have not minimised the suffering, down into the depths of a fiery Hell. It became better known when a farmer and dialect enthusiast, Bill Cowley, started the Lyke Wake Walk over this route in 1955. This popular walk of over forty miles across the North York Moors may even have its roots in pre-Christian Viking times, as suggested by such images in the dirge as that of the soul on the Day of Judgement passing over Whinny Moor (whinny is 'gorse') and crossing the narrow Brig o' Dreead (the Bridge of Dread).*

The Lyke Wake Dirge

This yah neet, this yah neet,
Ivvery neet an' all,
Fire an' fleet an' cann'l leet,
An' Christ tak up thi sawl.

When thoo fra hither gans away,
Ivvery neet an' all,
Ti Whinny Moor thoo cum'st at last,
An' Christ tak up thi sawl.

If ivver thoo gav' owther hosen or shoon,
Ivvery neet an' all,
Clap tha doon an' put 'em on,
An' Christ tak up thi sawl.

Bud if hosen or shoon thoo nivver ga' neean,
Ivvery neet an' all,
T' whinnies s'll prick thi sair ti t' beean,
An' Christ tak up thi sawl.

Fra Whinny Moor that thoo mayst pass,
Ivvery neet an' all,
Ti t' Brig o' Dreead thoo'll cum at last,
An' Christ tak up thi sawl.

But if o' siller an' gawd thoo nivver ga' neean,
Ivvery neet an' all,
Thoo'll doon, doon tumm'l tiwards Hell fleeams,
An' Christ tak up thi sawl.

Fra t' Brig o' Dreead 'at thoo mayst pass,
Ivvery neet an' all,
Ti t' fleeams o' Hell thoo'll cum at last,
An' Christ tak up thi sawl.

If ivver thoo gav' awther bite or sup,
Ivvery neet an' all,
T' fleeams'll nivver catch tha up,
An' Christ tak up thi sawl.

But if bite or sup thoo nivver ga' neean,
Ivvery neet an' all,
T' fleeams'll bo'n tha sair ti t' beean,
An' Christ tak up thi sawl.

*Another very old piece of dialect verse, of unknown date, is the little
poem which is traditionally recited at the Burning of Owd Bartle.
This takes place every year at West Witton in Wensleydale, on the
Saturday night nearest St Bartholomew's Day (24th August),
which may explain 'Bartle' as a corruption of Bartholomew —
though it is said he represents a man caught sheep-stealing, who has
to be punished. The effigy is carried shoulder-high through the village, with traditional stopping-places at homes and pubs, where
drinks are served to the carriers. Finally it is placed against a wall
at Grisgill End and set on fire to the accompaniment of singing and
the final shouting out of the following words, which have a touch of
almost prehistoric barbarity about them:*

Burning Owd Bartle

At Pen Hill crags
He tore his rags;
At Hunter's Horn
He blew his horn;
At Capplebank Stee
He brak his knee;
At Grisgill Beck
He brak his neck;
At Waddam's End
He couldn't fend
At Grisgill End
We'll mak his end:
Shout, lads, shout!

Burning Bartle, a unique custom held at West Witton, Wensleydale,
each August.

YORKSHIRE DIALECT CLASSICS

Much later than the Burning of Bartle, which is restricted to one village in Wensleydale, there is the burning of Guy Fawkes all over the county on Bonfire Night, commemorating his failure to blow up James I and the House of Lords on the 5th November 1605. Guy Fawkes was born in York in 1570, and lived as a young man at the secluded village of Scotton near Knaresborough, where he became a Catholic convert, and later joined the Spanish army, becoming a captain. So there is a special Yorkshire link with the Gunpowder Plot and the tradition still called in parts of the West Riding, 'Plot Neet'. Hence 'Plot Toffee' and such rhymes as the following, the first in Standard English, followed by reference to collecting wood — going chumpin' *or* proggin'.

Remember, remember the Fifth of November:
Gunpowder, treason and plot;
I see no reason
Why gunpowder treason
Should ever be forgot.

A stick and a stake,
For King James's sake!
Please give us a coil, a coil ...
An 'awpenny or a penny
Or else a black coil —
Or else we'll blaw yer
Aht o' t' 'oile! (WR)

Awd Grimey sits upon yon 'ill,
As black as onny awd craw;
He's getten on 'is long grey cooat,
Wi buttons doon afoare. (NR)

The custom of going round calling out Christmas greetings to friends and neighbours involved several rhymes, used especially by children begging a little Christmas box. Here are two from the North Riding, followed by the words of the wassail song from the West Riding, wassail being derived from the Anglo-Saxon Wes hal! (Good health!).

Ah wish yer a Merry Kessmas
An' a Happy New Year,

A pooakful o' money
An' a cellar-full o' beer;
A good fat pig
An' a new-cauven coo:
Good maisther an' mistheress,
Hoo do yer do?

God bless t' maisther o' this 'oose,
An' t' mistheress also,
An' all yer lahtle bonny bairns
'At roond yer teeable go!

A Christmas Wassail

Here we coom a-wessellin '
   Among the leaves so green,
An' here we coom a-wanderin'
   So fair as to be seen.

   Chorus —
   An' to your wessel
   An' to jolly wessel,
   Love an' joy be to you
   An' to your wessel-tree.

The wessel-bob is made
   O' rosemary tree,
An' so is your beer
   O' the best barley.
         An' to your wessel, etc.

We are not beggars' childeren
   That begs from door to door,
But we are neighbours' childeren
   That has been here before.
         An' to your wessel, etc.

We have got a little purse
   Made o' ratchin' leather skin,
An' we want a little money

To line it well within.
        An' to your wessel, etc.

Bring us out your table
    An' spread it wi' a cloth;
Bring us out your mouldy cheese
    Likewise your Christmas loaf.
        An' to your wessel, etc.

God bless the master o' this house,
    Likewise the mistress too;
An' all the little childeren
    That round the table go.
        An' to your wessel, etc.

Good master an' good misteress,
    While you're sittin' by the fire
Pray, think of us poor childeren
    That's wanderin' i' the mire.
        An' to your wessel, etc.

A Yorkshire Christmas pie, which traditionally consisted of a rich assortment of poultry together with seasoning, spices and butter.

Collected by Richard Blakeborough in the late nineteenth century, these lines are said to have been recited by a North Riding witch as she stirred into her pan grisly items such as a toad, frog, the heart of an ask *(newt), a dead man's teeth, in order to make a poisonous brew and work a curse. The date is unknown, but these lines powerfully convey a bygone age of primitive superstition.*

The Witch's Curse

Fire cum,
Fire gan,
Curling smeeak,
Keep oot o' t' pan.
Here's a teead, theer's a frog,
Here's t' heart frev a crimson ask

As streight as a yard o' pump-watter.

Here's a teeath fra t' heead
O' yan at's deead,
'At nivver gat thruff his task;
Here's pricked i' blood a maiden's prayer
'At t' ee o' man maunt see;
It's pricked reeght thruff a yet warm mask,
An' lapt aboot a breet green ask:,
An' it's all for him an' thee.
   It boils,
   thoo'll drink!
   He'll speeak,
   tho'll think!
   It boils,
   thoo'll see!
   He'll speeak,
   thoo'll dee! (NR)

David Lewis was the first named Yorkshire dialect poet of real merit to have his poems printed in a book. A farmer at Belmont, between Harrogate and Knaresborough, he was largely self-educated, working for a time as a schoolmaster and accountant. In 1815 he published The Landscape and Other Poems, *including the two following poems in North Riding dialect. The first is obviously influenced by Robert Burns and his reaction to having disturbed a mouse. Here Lewis reflects that, like the frog he has accidentally killed, we shall all be cut down by the relentless scythe of time. The second poem is also about an actual incident involving a soot-blackened boy working for a chimney-sweep, whose sudden appearance makes him seem like* Awd Nick *(the Devil).*

Elegy on the Death of a Frog

Ya summer day when I were mowin',
When flooers of monny soorts were growin',

Which fast befoor my scythe fell bowin',
   As I advance,
A frog I cut widout my knowin'
   A sad mischance.

Poor luckless frog, why com thoo here?
Thoo sure were destitute o' fear;
Some other way could thoo nut steer
   To shun the grass?
For noo that life, which all hod dear,
   Is geean, alas!

Hadst thoo been freeten'd by the soond
With which the mowers strip the groond,
Then fled away wi' nimble boond,
   Thoo'd kept thy state:
But I, unknawin', gav a wound,
   Which browt thy fate.

Sin thoo com frae thy parent spawn,
Wi' painted cooat mair fine than lawn,
And golden rings round baith ees drawn,
   All gay an' blithe,
Thoo lowpt the fields like onny fawn,
   But met the scythe.

Frae dikes where winter watters steead
Thoo com unto the dewy mead,
Regardless of the cattle's treead,
   Wi' pantin' breeath,
For to restore thy freezin' bleead,
   But met wi' deeath.

A Frenchman early seekin' prog,
Will oftentimes ransack the bog,
To finnd a sneel, or well-fed frog,
    To give relief;
But I prefer a leg of hog,
    Or roond o' beef.

But liker far to the poor frog,
I's wanderin' through the world for prog,
Where deeath gies monny a yan a jog,
    An' cuts them doon;
An' though I think missen incog,
    That way I's boun.

Time whets his scythe and shakes his glass,
And though I know all flesh be grass,
Like monny mair I play the ass,
    Don't seem to know;
But here wad sometime langer pass,
    Befoor I go.

Ye bonnie lasses, livin' flooers,
Of cottage mean, or gilded booers,
Possessèd of attractive pooers,
    Ye all mun gang
Like frogs in meadows fed by shooers,
    Ere owt be lang.

Though we to stately plants be grown,
He easily can mow us doon;
It may be late, or may be soon,
    His scythe we feel;
Or is it fittin' to be known?
    Therefore fareweel.

David Lewis (NR)

The Sweeper and the Thieves

A sweeper's lad was late o' t' neet,
His slape-shod shun had leeam'd his feet;
He call'd ti see a good awd deeame,
'At monny a time had trigg'd his wame,
For he wor then fahve miles fra yam:
He ax'd i' t' lair ti let him sleep,
An' he'd next day, ther chimlers sweep.
They supper'd him wi' country fare,
Then show'd him tul his hooal i' t' lair.
He crept intul his streay bed,
His poak o' seeat beneath his heead;
He wor content, nur car'd a pin,
An' his good frind then lock'd him in.
The lair fra t' hoose a distance stood,
Between 'em grew a lahtle wood:
Aboot midneet, or nearer moorn,
Two thieves brak in ti steeal ther coorn;
Heving a leet i' lantern dark,
They seean ti winder fell ti wark;
And wishin' they'd a lad to fill,
Young Brush (wheea yet had ligg'd quite still)
Thinkin' 'at t' men belang'd ti t' hoose
An' that he noo mud be of use,
Jump'd doon directly on ti t' fleear
An' t' thieves then beath ran oot o' t' deear,
Nor stopt at owt, nur thin, nur thick,
Fully convinced it wor Awd Nick.
The sweeper lad then ran reet seean
Ti t' hoose, an' tell'd 'em what wor deean:
Maister an' men then quickly raise,
An' ran ti t' lair wi' hoaf ther clais.
Twea horses, secks, an' leet they fand,
Which had been left by t' thievish band;
These roond i' t' neybourheead they cry'd

Yorkshire's mills and canals — a once-prosperous combination.

But nut an awner e'er apply'd,
For neean durst horses awn, or secks,
They wor se freeten'd o' ther necks;
Yan horse an' seck wor judg'd t' sweeper's share,
Because he kept t' farmer's coorn an' lair.

David Lewis (NR)

John Castillo (1792-1845) was born near Dublin, but grew up at Lealholm Bridge, on the moors near Whitby. He became a stonemason, and a Methodist local preacher and poet, well-known all over North Yorkshire. Before he could read and write he composed the thirty stanzas of Awd Isaac, *dictating them to a friend. Just the conclusion is quoted here, including the last verse, which is inscribed on Castillo's tombstone at Pickering.*

Awd Isaac

Oft hev Ah lang'd yon hill ti clim,
Ti hev a bit mare prooase wi' him
Wheas coonsel like a pleasing dreeam,
Is deear ti me;
Sin' roond the warld sike men as he
Seea few ther be.

Corrupted bewks he did detest,
For his wur of the varry best;
This meead him wiser than the rest
O' t' neeaburs roond,
Tho' poor e' purse, wi' senses blest
An' judgment soond.

Befoore the silvery neet ov age,
The precepts ov the sacred page
His meditation did engage,
That race ti run;
Like thooase, who 'spite o' Satan's rage,
The prahze hed won.

Bud noo his een 's geean dim i' deeath,
Neea mare a pilgrim here on eearth,
His sowl flits fra' her shell beneeath,
Ti realms o' day
Whoor carpin care, an' pain, an' deeath,
Are deean away.

John Castillo (NR)

A grass-roots product of the steel industry in South Yorkshire, and especially Sheffield, this poem was written by Abel Bywater, founder of the first-known almanack published entirely in dialect, the Wheelswarf Chronicle *(1830). It concerns men forging knives known as* flat-backs, *who are about to slake their thirst and go off to the dance known as the* penny-hop.

Sheffield Cutler's Song

Coom all you cutlin' heroes, where'ersome 'er you be,
All you what works at flat-backs, coom listen unto me;
    A basketful for a shillin',
    To mak 'em we are willin',
Or swap 'em for red herrin's, aar bellies to be fillin',
Or swap 'em for red herrin's, aar bellies to be fillin'.

A basketful o' flat-backs, I'm sure we'll mak, or more,
To ger reight into t' gallery, wheer we can rant an' roar,
    Throw flat-backs, stones an' sticks,
    Red herrin's, bones an' bricks,
If they don't play 'Nancy's fancy' or onny tune we fix,
We'll do the best at e'er we can to break some o' their necks.

Hey! Jont, lad, is that thee, where art ta waddlin' to?
Does ta work at flat-backs yit, as tha's been used to do?
    Ho! coom, an' tha s'go wi' me,
    An' a sample I will gie thee,
It's one 'at I've just forged upon Geoffry's bran' new stiddy.
Look at it well, it does excel all t' flat-backs i' aar smithy.

Let's send for a pitcher o' ale, lad, for I'm gerrin' varry droy,
I'm ommost chok'd wi' smithy sleck, the wind it is so hoigh.
    Gie Rafe an' Jer a drop,
    They sen they cannot stop,
They're i' sich a moighty hurry to get to t' penny hop,
They're i' sich a moighty hurry to get to t' penny hop.

Abel Bywater (WR)

Ben Preston (1819-1902) was born in Bradford, the son of a hand-loom weaver, and became a wool-sorter. Though he later lived at Bingley, and then Eldwick, celebrating the countryside, he was very familiar with the hard work, injustice and poverty involved in the textile trade. Facing up to the shame of a baby being born out of wedlock, here a grandmother addresses the child as doy, *a West Riding term of affection, like 'dear'.*

Come to thi Granny, Doy

Come to thi Gronny, doy! come to thi Gronny!
Bless tha, to me tha'rt as precious as onny;
Mutherless barn of a dowter unwed,
Little tha knaws, doy, the tears 'at Ah've shed;
Trials Ah've knawn booath fur t' heart an' fur t' heead,
Shortness o' wark, aye, an' shortness o' breead.

Thease Ah could bide, bud tho' tha'rt nooan to blame,
Bless tha, tha browt ma booath sorrow an' shame;
Gronny, poor sowl, fur a two-munth or mooare
Hardly could feshion to lewk aht o' t' dooar;
T' neighbours called aht to ma, 'Dunnot stand that,
Aht wi' that hussy, an' aht wi' hur brat!'

Deary me, deary me, what could Ah say?
T' first thing of all, Ah thowt, 'Let ma gooa pray.'
T' next time Ah slept Ah'd a dream de ya see,
Aye, an' Ah knew 'at that dream wur fur me:
Tears o' Christ Jesus, Ah saw 'em that neet,
Fall drop be drop onta one at His feet.

After that, saw Him wi' barns rahnd His knee,
Some on 'em, happen, poor crayturs like thee;
Says Ah at last, though Ah sorely wur tried,
Suarly a sinner, a sinner sud bide;
Neighbours may think or may say what they will,
T' muther an' t' dowter sal stop wi' ma still.

A woman's work is never done. (Throng as Throp's wife.)

Come on't what will, i' mi cot they sal cahr,
Woe be to them 'at maks bad inta wahr;
Some fowk may call tha a name 'at Ah hate,
Wishing fro t' heart tha wur weel aht o' t' gate;
Oft this hard world inta t' gutter 'll shove tha,
Poar little lamb, wi' no daddy ta luve tha.

Dunnot thee freeat, doy, whol Gronny hods up,
Nivver sal tha want a bite or a sup;
What if Ah wark theease owd fingers ta t' boan,
Happen tha'll luve ma long after Ah'm gooan.
T' last bite i' t' cupboard wi' thee Ah could share't
Hay! bud tha's stown a rare slice o' my heart.

Spite o' all t' sorra, all t' shame at Ah've seen,
Sunshine comes back to mi heart throo thi een;
Cuddle thi Gronny, doy; Bless tha, tha'rt bonny, doy,
Rosy an' sweet, thro thi brah to thi feet,
Kingdoms an' crahns wodn't buy tha ta-neet!

Ben Preston (WR)

Samuel Laycock (1826-93) was born in Marsden, close to the border with Lancashire, which claims him as one of their own dialect poets. However, the experience of unemployment in the textile area immediately associates him with writers like Ben Preston, John Hartley and others, as is shown in this poem about a baby born into a poverty-stricken home. They are so poor that they can hardly afford to give pobbies *(bread soaked in milk) to an older child being weaned.*

Welcome, bonny Brid

Tha'rt welcome, little bonny brid,
But shouldn't ha' come just when tha did;
Toimes are bad.
We're short o' pobbies for eawr Joe,
But that, of course, tha didn't know,
Did ta, lad?...

Aw've often yeard mi feyther tell,
'At when Aw coom i' th' world missel,
Trade wur slack;
And neaw it's hard wark pullin' thoo —
But Aw munnot fear thee — iv Aw do
Tha'll go back.

God bless thi, love! Aw'm fain tha'rt come,
Just try and mak thissel at hooam:
Here's thi nest;

Tha'rt loike thi mother to a tee,
But tha's thi feyther's nose, Aw see,
Well, Aw'm blest!

Come, come, tha needn't look so shy,
Aw am no' blamin thee, not I;
Settle deawn,
An tak this hawp'ny for thisel',
Ther's lots o' sugar-sticks to sell
Deawn i' th' teawn.

Aw knaw when first Aw coom to th' leet,
Aw're fond o' owt 'at tasted sweet;
Tha'll be t' same.
But come, tha's nivver towd thi Dad
What he's to call thi yet, mi lad,
What's thi name?

Hush! Hush! Tha mustn't cry this way,
But get this sup o' cinder tay
While it's wahrm;
Mi mother used to give it me,
When Aw wur sich a lad as thee,
In her arm.

Hush-a-babby, hush-a-bee, —
Oh, what a temper! — dear-i-me
Heaw tha skrikes!
Here's a bit o sugar, sithee;
Howd thi noise, an then aw'll gie thee
Owt tha likes.

We've nobbut getten coarsish fare,
But, eawt o' this tha'll get thi share
Nivver fear.
Aw hope tha'll nivver want a meal,
But allus fill thi belly weel
While tha'rt here.

Thi feyther's nooan been wed so long,
An yet tha sees he's middlin throng
Wi yo o'.
Besides thi little brother Ted
We've one upsteers, asleep i' bed,
Wi eawr Joe.

But tho we've childer two or three
We'll mak a bit o' reeawm for thee,
Bless thee, lad!
Th'art th' prattiest brid we have i' th' nest
So hutch up closer to mi breast...
Aw'm thi Dad.

Samuel Laycock (WR)

On Ilkla Mooar Baht At *is the best-known dialect song in the world, with the possible exception of 'Auld Lang Syne'. Yet, although the words are authentic West Riding dialect, they are sung to a tune written, not in Yorkshire, but in Kent, a hymn-tune, in fact, composed by a Canterbury boot and shoe-maker and conductor of Methodist choirs, Thomas Clark. He published it in 1805, naming it 'Cranbrook' after the market town on the Weald, and it is typical of the tunes used by Methodists, who had been encouraged by John Wesley to 'sing lustily'.*

Some time in the second half of the nineteenth century there was a choir outing over Ilkley Moor (the strongest contenders are from the Ebeneezer Primitive Methodist Chapel, Halifax), during which a couple wandered away from the main party. When they returned the young man had his leg pulled by his friends, who called out their jibes a line at a time ... Where was he wandering off to without his hat? (Everybody wore a hat in those days.) He'd been for a romp in the heather. That was it! He'd been courting Mary Jane. He'd get his death of cold ... And so on. It was quite natural for them to make their jests in dialect — and to find themselves singing them to one of the favourite hymn-tunes they knew by heart. Just a bit of fun, but their jest and the name of Ilkley Moor have been carried all round the world by a simple but memorable melody.

It was first published in Huddersfield in 1916, but the collector C H Dennis claimed it had been sung for at least two generations. His version is of a mother asking her son what he's been up to on the moor ('Ah 'll tell thi fatther when 'e comes 'ooam!') But it is roughly the same as the following, which has become the standard:

On Ilkla Mooar baht 'at

1 Wheeare wo' ta bahn when Ah saw thee
   On Ilkla Mooar baht 'at?

2 Tha's been a-coourtin' Mary Jane
   On Ilkla Mooar baht 'at.

As cheerful as a chapel lowsin'.

3 Tha's bahn ter get thi deeath o' cowd
  On Ilkla Mooar baht 'at.

4 Then wi s'll 'a ' ter bury thee
  On Ilkla Mooar baht 'at.

5 Then t' wurrums 'll come an' eyt thee up
  On Ilkla Mooar baht 'at.

6 Then t' ducks 'll come an' eyt up t' wurrums
  On Ilkla Mooar baht 'at.

7 Then wi s'll come an' eyt up t' ducks
  On Ilkla Mooar baht 'at.

8 Then wi s'll all 'ave etten thee
  On Ilkla Mooar baht 'at.

9 That's wheeare wi get us ooan back!
  On Ilkla Mooar baht 'at.

John Hartley (1839-1915) is undoubtedly the most prolific and popular of all the early writers of West Riding dialect. Earlier generations knew his poems by heart, and — following Hartley's own example on stage — they were regularly given as public recitations. Living in Leeds, Bradford and London, he settled in Halifax, where he founded the famous Clock Almanack *in 1865. Selling as many as 120,000 copies each year, it was published annually until 1957. In the early years Hartley wrote much of the material himself, showing that he was a lively bohemian character, and a champion of the ordinary folk who toiled away in the mill-towns. He published several collections of his poems. These range from comic verse, such as* Ahr Mary's Bonnet *(once so well-known that garbled versions about 'Ahr Sal's bonnet' survive), poems about work in the woollen mills (better than* laikin', *being unemployed) and through love poems such as* Nelly o' Bob's, *to moving protests about children living in the abject poverty of industrial areas, such as my own favourite* A Ha'porth, *the story of how a little halfpenny coin could make all the difference.*

Ahr Mary's Bonnet

Have yo seen awr Mary's bonnet?
    It's a stunner — nooa mistak!
Ther's a bunch o' rooasies on it,
    An' a feather daan her back.
Yollo ribbons an' fine laces,
    An' a cock-a-doodle-doo,
An' raand her bonny face is
    A string o' pooasies blue.

When shoo went to church last Sundy,
    T' parson could'nt finnd his text;
An' fat old Mistress Grundy
    Sed, 'Eh, Mary! pray what next!'
T' lads wink'd at one another —
    T' lasses snikered i' ther glee,
An' t' whooal o' t' congregation
    Had her bonnet i' ther ee.

Sooin t' singers started singin',
    But they braik daan one bi one,
For t' hymn wor on 'The flowers
    Of fifty summers gone.',
But when they saw awr Mary,
    They made a mullock on it,
For they thowt' at all them flaars
    Had been put on Mary's bonnet.

Then t' parson said mooast kindly,
    'Ther wor noa offence intended;
But flaar shows wor aht o' place,
    I' t' church wheeare saints attended.
An' if his errin sister wished
    To finnd her way to glory;

Shoo shouldn't carry on her heead,
　　A whooal consarvatory.'

Nah, Mary isn't short o' pluck —
　　Shoo jumpt up in a minnit,
Shoo lukt as if shoo'd swollo t' church,
　　An' ivverybody in it.
'Parson,' shoo said, 'yor heead is bare —
　　Nowt in it an' nowt on it;
Suppooas yo put some flaars thear,
　　Like theease 'at's in my bonnet.'

John Hartley (WR)

Waivin' Mewsic

Ther's mewsic in t' shuttle, in t' loom, an' in t' frame,
Ther's melody mingled in t' noise;
For t' active ther's praises, for t' idle ther's blame,
If the'd harken to t' saand of its voice,
An' when flaggin' a bit, how refreshin' to feel,
As you pause an' look raand on the throng,
At the clank o' the tappet, the hum o' the wheel,
Sing this plain unmistakable song:
　　Nick a ting, nock a ting;
　　Wages keep pocketin';
Workin' for little is better nor laikin';
　　Twist an' twine, reel an' wind;
　　Keep a contented mind;
Troubles are oft of a body's own makin' ...

An then see what lessons are laid out anent us,
As pick after pick follows time after time,
An' warns us, tho' silent, to let nowt prevent us
From strivin' by little endeavours to climb;
T' world's made o' trifles, its dust forms a mountain,

Then nivver despair as yor trudgin' along;
If troubles will come an' yor spirits dishearten,
Yo'll finnd ther's relief i' that steady owd song:
   Nick a ting, nock a ting;
   Wages keep pocketin';
Workin' for little is better nor laikin;
   Twist an twine, reel an wind;
   Keep a contented mind;
Troubles are oft of a body's own makin'.

John Hartley (WR)

A laithe, a typical barn of the Yorkshire Dales.

Nelly o' Bobs

Who is it 'at lives i' that cot on the lea?
Joy o' mi heart, an' leet o' mi ee;
Who is that lass at's soa dear unto me?
Nelly o' Bob's o' t' Crowtrees.

Who is it goes trippin o'er dew-spangled grass,
Singin so sweetly? Shoo smiles as Aw pass;
Bonniest, rooasy-cheek'd, gay-hearted lass!
Nelly o' Bob's o' t' Crowtrees.

Who is it Aw see i' mi dreeams of a neet?
Who lovinly whispers words tender an' sweet
Till Aw wakken to find 'at shoo's nowheeare i' t' seet?
Nelly o' Bob's o' t' Crowtrees.

Who is it 'at leeads me soa lively a donce,
Yet to talk serious ne'er gies me a chonce,
An' nivver replied when Aw begged on her once?
Nelly o' Bob's o' t' Crowtrees.

Who is it ivvery chap's hank'rin' to get,
Yet tosses her heead an' flies off in a pet;
As mich as to say, 'Yo've net getten me yet!'
Nelly o' Bob's o' t' Crowtrees.

Who is it could mak life a long summer's day,
Whose smile wod drive sorrow an' trouble away;
An' mak t' hardest wark, if for her, seem like play?
Nelly o' Bob's o' t' Crowtrees.

Who is it Aw'll have if Aw've ivver a wife,
An' love her, her only, to t' end o' mi life,
An' nurse her i' sickness, an' guard her from strife?
Nelly o' Bob's o' t' Crowtrees.

Who is it 'at's promised, to-neet, if its fine,
To meet me at t' corner o' t' mistal at nine?
Why, its her 'at Aw've langed for sooa long to mak mine—
Nelly o' Bob's o' t' Crowtrees.

John Hartley (WR)

A Hawporth

Wheear is thi daddy, doy? Wheeare is thi mam?
What are ta cryin for, poor little lamb?
Dry up thi peepies, pet, wipe thi wet face;
Tears on thy little cheeks seem aht o' place.
What do they call thi, lad? Tell me thi name;
Have they been ooinin' thi? Why, it's a shame!
Here, tak this hawpny, an' buy thi some spice,
Rocksticks or humbugs or summat 'at's nice.
Then run off hooam ageean, fast as tha can;
Theeare — tha'rt all reight ageean; run like a man!

He wiped up his tears wi' his little white brat,
An' he tried to say summat, Aw couldn't tell what:
But his little face breeten'd wi' pleasure all throo: —
Eh! — it's cappin, sometimes, what a hawpny can do.

John Hartley (WR)

Thomas Blackah (1828-95) was another almanack editor and writer, born on Greenhow Hill, becoming a leadminer and spending most of his life at Pateley Bridge, where he published T' Nidderdale Olminac. *His local dialect, though from not far north of the West Riding, is distinctly North Riding.*

Pateley Reeaces

Attention all, baith great an' small,
    An' dooan't screw up yer feeaces;
While I rehearse, i' simple verse,
    A coont o' Pateley Reeaces.

Fra all ower t' moors, they com bi scoores
    Girt skelpin' lads an' lasses;
An' cats an' dogs, an' coos an' hogs,
    An' hosses, mules, an' asses.

Oade foaks wer thar, fra near an' far
   'At cuddant fairly hopple;
An' laughin' brats, as wild as cats,
   Ower heeads an' heels did topple.

The Darley lads, arrived i' squads,
   Wi' smiles all ower ther feeaces,
An' Hartwith youths, wi' screw'd-up mooths
   In wonder watch'd the reeaces.

Fra Menwith Hill, and Folly Gill,
   Thorntyat, an' Deacre Paster,
Fra Thruscross Green, an' t' Heets wer seen
   Croods cumin' thick an' faster.

'Tween Bardin Brigg and Threshfield Rig
   Oade Wharfedeeale gat a thinnin';
An' Gerston plods laid heavy odds
   On Creeaven Lass fer winnin'.

Sich lots were seen o' Hebdin Green,
   Ready seean on i' t' mornin',
While Aptrick chaps, i' carts an' traps,
   Wer offta Patela' spornin.

All Greenho' Hill, past Coadsteeanes kill,
   Com toltherin' an' singin'
Harcastle coves, like sheep i' droves,
   Oade Palmer Simp wer bringin'.

Baith short an' tall, past Gowthit Halll,
   T' up-deealers kept on steerin',
For ne'er before, roond Middlesmoor,
   Had ther been sich a clearin'.

All kinds and sorts o' games an' sports
   Had t' Patela' chaps pervided,
An' weel did t' few, ther business do,
   At ower 'em persided.

'Twad tak a swell a munth ta tell
   All t' ins an' oots o' t' reeaces.

A Dales shepherd, with a 'yowe' and her lambs.

Hoo far the' ran, which hosses wan,
　　An' which wer' back'd for pleeaces …

An' when at last the sports were past,
　　All heeamward turn'd ther feeaces;
Ta ne'er relent at e'er the' spent
　　A day wi' Patela' Reeaces.

Thomas Blackah (NR)

Pleeaf Stots (Plough Bullocks) is a North Riding term for the men who performed a traditional sword dance on Plough Monday — the first Monday after Epiphany, when work on the farms was resumed after the Christmas break. The plough was pulled round the villages by the lively stots, who performed their long-sword dance, asking for gifts of drink or money — and sometimes ploughed a furrow in front of an inhospitable house. The brightly-costumed dancers included t' Oad (old) Man and t' Oad Woman, and the climax of the dance was the skilled weaving of the swords into a lock *(*'Watch 'em plet at last their sooards'*) which is held aloft — a symbol perhaps of the sun rising again after the winter solstice. FW Dowson, born in Goathland on the North York Moors, here describes the old dance in his village, revived by him at the suggestion of Cecil Sharp in 1923.*

T' Pleeaf Stots

Here they cum, tidaay seea grand,
Runnin', lowpin', sooards i' hand:
Rooases, ribbins, cooats seea sthraange,
Hoose ti hoose they're gahin' ti raange.

Last back-end when neets was dark,
All t' lads set theirsens ti wark—
Leearnt their steps, an' showed their airt,
Watchin' t' oad foaks deea their pairt.

Hoo they thried an' thried ageean,
Thowt this nivver wad be deean!
Then they dhrissed i' sike fine cleease,
Fancy suits frae heead ti teeas.

'Blews' an' 'pinks' is allus pets:
Seean theease danced i' tweea fine sets.
Watch 'em plet at last their sooards,
Just when theease seeam flung all rooads!

Here's t' Oad Woman, an' t' Oad Man!
Peeak'd aboon 'em sits a cloon.
Sike queer 'stots', an' actin' teea,
Sum on deearsteean, sum i' t' fleear!

Off they gan awaay ower t' green,
Sike a show, was't ivver seen?
Noo they're i' t' foad-garth ti start,
Iw'ry yan seea glad at heart.

Watch their antics whaal they're there!
Neean bud what is straight an' fair:
Hoo they dance, an' stand up fine,
Just like soldiers iv a line.

All their wods they just fit reet,
And their pairts all suits their feet;
Fost they dance wi' sooards on end,
Then they clap 'em doon an' bend.

Roond an' roond they dance i' t' ring,
Then they talks and sumtahmes sing:
Grand oad fiddler! Wheea can beat
Times like thine is despert greeat ...

Laugh an' dance, an' shoot an' sing!
This is t'daay ti hae yer fling:

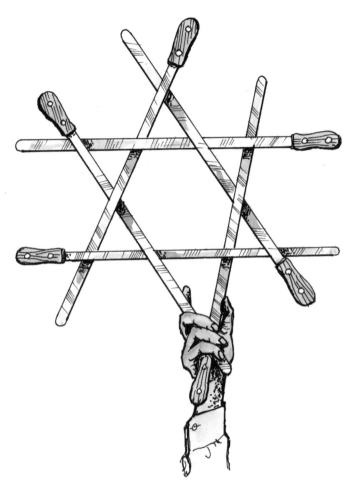

The 'lock' held aloft as the climax of a longsword dance, such as that performed at Goathland: 'Watch 'em plet at last their sooards'.

Keep t'oad plaay up ivv'ry year,
Nowt else like it, we're all seear.

All you lads at's leeakin' on,
Tak yer to'ns — git t' jackets on!
Deea like t' oad-uns — keep it up;
When it's ower'd fill yer cup!

F W Dowson (NR)

This poem captures the joyful springtime scene of lambs frisking about in the fields and fells of Wensleydale. One of many poems written by John Thwaite (1873-1941), born at West Burton, near Aysgarth, a grocer at Hawes and a lover of his native dale.

Layky Lambs

A snyzy day, a cowd Eeast wind,
But lambs mun stretch the'r legs, ye'll finnd,
I' April's fickle weather;
It's bin a hardish neet, bi t' hime,
It's cappen hoo they stand this clime,
The're meeastly teuf as leather.

When t' sun gits oot it's time fer t' spoorts,
They cut some capers, teu, aw' soorts,
The're aw' i' tip-top fettle;
Ther's yan fast doonhill, yan's a climmer,
A bonny, booncen, black-feeaced gimmer,
They fairly show the'r mettle ...

T' yowes cheg away, gey thrang, hard by,
T' lambs bump back te the'r mothers, dry;
They want neea milkin' pails.
Weel under t' flanks the'r heids they dook,

Hoo greedily they grep an' sook;
Noo watch them waggen tails!

An' ivvery yowe kna's just what's what,
Sha wants ni other owd deeame's brat;
Nay, nowt but what's her ahn!
At times it meeans a blate, a gliff,
Er mebbe noo an' than a sniff,
T' lile tykes seun git weel knahn.

John Thwaite (NR)

Infant mortality was one of the commonest and most harrowing experiences before the advent of effective modern medical aid. Here William Wright (1836-97), a poetic warp-dresser, who wrote under the pen-name of 'Bill o' th' Hoylus End' (a village between Keighley and Howarth), powerfully conveys the anguish of losing his little boy.

Cowd as Leead

An' arta fra thi fatther torn
So early i' thi youthful morn,
An' mun Ah pine away forlorn
I' grief an' pain?
For consolashun Ah sall scorn
If tha be ta'en.

Oh, yes, tha art, an' Ah mun wail
Thi loss through ivvery hill an' dale,
Fer nah it is too true a tale,
Tha'rt cowd as leead.
An' nah thi bonny face is pale,
Tha'rt deead! Tha'rt deead!

Ah miss tha when Ah cum fra t' shop,
An' see thi bat, an' ball, an' top;
An' Ah's be ommost fit ta drop,

Ah sall so freeat;
An' Oh! Mi varry heart may stop
An' cease to beeat!

Ah allus aimed, if tha'd been spared,
Of summat better to hev shared,
Ner what thi poor owd father fared,
I' this cowd sphere;
Yet, after all, Ah s't nooan 'a' cared
If tha'd stayed here.

But O! Tha Conqueror Divine,
'At vanquished deeath i' Palestine,
Tak to thi arms this lad o' mine,
Nooan freely given;
But mak him same as wun o' thine
Wi' Thee i' Heaven.

William Wright (WR)

Nowadays, when farms are under threat and many are closing, it is remarkable to see in this anonymous song from mid-Victorian times a farmer from the Ampleforth area carrying on about the weather, and fearing he'd breeak *(go bankrupt).*

A Yorkshire Farmer's Lament

Rainin' ageean Ah deea declare;
It's twaa days wet for yah day fair;
Warse tahmes than theease was nivver seen,
Us farmers 'll be beggar'd clean.

Crops is seea bad Ah's varra flay'd
Rents, rates, an' taxes can't be paid;
Harvest foaks' wages gannin' on,
An' there the' stand, an' nowt is done.

What a sad mess o' mouldy hay,
An' taaties rottin' all awaa:
Wheeat thin o' t' grund, an' small i' t' ear,
It caan't yield weel, Ah's varra seear ...

There's nowt te eeat for milkin' kye
An' meeast on 'em 'll seean be dry;
Tahmes noo for farmers is seea bad,
Ye'll see next spring the'll breeak like mad.

anon (NR)

*F Austin Hyde, a grammar school headmaster born at Driffield in
1889, and a fluent speaker of his native dialect, in these two poems
pays eloquent tribute to a farmer's old mare and a shepherd's old
sheepdog.*

Depper, Awd Meer

Hev Ah onny awd 'osses, young fellow frev 'Ull?
Thoo's willin' tae buy 'em, gie value i' full?
Why yis, Ah have yan, i' this paddock doon here,
Cohip, then! Coom on, then! Coom, Depper, awd meer!

No, she dizn't coom gallopin', bud then, you see,
Meer's a bit wankle like, tonned twenty-three.
Thoo'll mebbe not be quite sae frisky thissen
When thoo's seen thi greeat-grandsons grow up tae be men!

Weel, what will Ah tak for her? Why noo, she's fat,
An' they tell me you give a bit extry for that,
Bud Ah might as well tell tha, thoo'll not buy that meer
If thoo stands there an' bids me fra noo tae next year.

She was t' fost fooal Ah 'ad when Ah com' upo'd place,
An' fost she's been allus, i' shaft, pole or thrace.
She's ploughed, drilled an' harrowed, rolled, scruffled an' led,
An' mothered Beaut, Boxer, Prince, Cobby an' Ned.

If threshin' machine gat stuck fast on its way,
Young 'osses wad plunge, rahve an' tew hauf o'd day,
Bud afoor it gat shifted it allus was 'Here, Away thoo gans,
Thoddy, an' fetch us t'awd meer!'

YORKSHIRE DIALECT CLASSICS

When stacks was afire, afoor motor car days,
She galloped tae Driffield when t' spot was ablaze,
Ovver field, ditch and hedgerow for t' gainest way doon,
Saved buildings, an' hoos an' three pikes, Ah'll be boon!

When t' missus took badly, when t' babby was born,
'Twas a life an' deeath jonny for t' doctor that morn,
An' though she'd been workin' at t' plough all day lang
T' meer galloped as tho' she knew summat was wrang.

Wi' never a whip, not a jerk on her rein,
She went like a whirlwind an' flew back again,
Wi' t' doctor an' nuss, just i' time tae save life —
Aye, Depper, Ah owe thoo baith dowter an' wife.

On friends 'at's sae faithfill we dooan't turn wer backs,
Nor send 'em for slaughter tae'd foreigner's axe,
Nor let 'em be worked tae their deeath across t' sea,
Wheer nivver a Yorkshire voice shouts 'Wahve' nor 'Gee'.

The Cleveland Bay — a fine all-purpose Yorkshire breed.

No, noo 'at she's neither young, bonny nor soond,
She awns t' lahtle paddock, it's pensioner's groond,
An' stall i' yon stable, hay, beddin' an' corn,
Ah reckon she's addled a spot of her awn!

An' when the day comes 'at we do hae tae pairt,
She'll gan in a way 'at 'll not brek her hairt,
An' t' land 'at she's worked on an' loved twenty year
At last'll lig leet on my faithfill awd meer.

F Austin Hyde (ER)

A Yorkshire Shepherd to his Dog

Seea thoo's parzelled thi way in ageean, awd dog,
    Thoo's parzelled thi way in ageean?
Thoo knaws varry weel at Ah've getten mi tea,
Seea thoo cums nuzzlin up ti t' firesahd ti me
Wi t' seeam faithful lewk i thi bonny broon ee,
    Seeam lewk i thi bonny broon ee.

Thoo knaws ivvry wod at Ah say, awd dog,
    Thoo was nivver yan ti tell twice;
A wave or a shoot or a whistle ti thoo,
Thoo'd be off iv a quicksticks wheer t' wark war ti do;
Fleet o' foot, keen o' brain, allus loyal an trew,
    Aye, thoo's allus bin loyal an trew.

When t' snawstorm cum doon thick an fast durin t' neet,
    An t' sheeap was all buried on t'moor,
It war thoo at knawed just wheer ivvry yan lay,
As wa toiled, up ti t'oxters, bi t' fost leet o' day;
Thoo browt ivvry yan on em safely away,
    Ivvry yan on 'em safely away.

When t' killer war oot up o' t' moor, awd dog,
    Runnin wild up o' t' moor amang t'sheeap,

Wheea fought for mi lambs fre dusk awhahl dawn,
An cum back i dayleet all bleedin' an torn?
Bud nivver a yowe left forlorn, awd dog,
   Bud nivver a yowe left forlorn.

Passon sez at thoo esn't a sowl, awd dog,
   'E sez at thoo esn't a sowl!
'E's a far-larnt man, a deal wiser nor me,
Wiv is Greek an' is Ebrew an' Theologee;
Bud 'e knaws nowt at all aboot dogs sike as thee,
   'E knaws nowt aboot dogs sike as thee!

Ah read for missen i t'Awd Book of a neet,
   Aye, Ah read i' t' owd Book ivvry neet,
An' a Greater than him, at loved beeath man an' beast,
Biddin them on his right hand ti t' Heavenly Feast,
Said 'Well done!" for being faithful i' things that was least.
   Thoo's been faithful i' things that was least.

We're beeath on us wankle an' wemmly an awd,
   Oor flittin-tahm's boun ti cum seean.
Thoo's fought a good fight, lad; thoo's run a straight reeace.
Good Shipperd wad nivver shut t' deear i' thi feeace.
Nay! Aboon i' green pasturs 'E'll finnd thoo a pleeace.
Ah awp at 'E'll finnd yan for me, awd dog,
   Ah awp 'at 'E'll finnd yan for me!

F Austin Hyde (ER)

Dorothy Una Ratcliffe (Mrs McGregor Phillips), a children's writer and a leading light of the Yorkshire Dialect Society, wrote many dialect poems about her native North Yorkshire. Here is one of her love poems.

Cock-leet

It's nobbut cock-leet, Sweetheart! Hast come by Yorla Moor?
Whya, Lad! thoo mun be famished! I' Muther's cheeany crock
Are spice-loaves an' fat-rascals! Dost hear my Father snore?
Hark! Half-past four a-soundin' fra' Yorla tower clock!

Whisht noo! Gie ower cuddlin', Lad, an' doan't be sae rough!
I'se t' cows to milk, t' butter to kurn, an' tak' to Dunnel Brigg.
Yet I'se fain to gan sweetheartin' up bonnie Altor Cleugh,
Forgittin' a' but thee an' me, by t' birks o' Wyresal Rigg,

Wheer t' moortops are a-ringin' wi' t' canty lilt o' t' lark,
Wheer foxes hide i' brekkons an' t'grass is rare to tread;
Ay, Lad, I'll coom sweetheartin' wi' thee at t' edge o' dark.
But wark's to do at cock-leet, an' my folk are still a-bed!

Dorothy Una Ratcliffe (NR)

Wilfrid J Halliday, born in Pudsey, was joint editor of the White
Rose Garland *(1949) and made an outstanding contribution to
the Yorkshire Dialect Society, serving as chairman (1946-64), and
president (1964-74). The first of these poems takes its title from the
dialect word for marriage banns.*

T' Spurrins

They've putten in t' spurrins, they're bahn to be wed,
    An' shoo'll be a reight bonny brahd.
Shoo's dimpled an' roasy, wi cheeks near as red
    As t'mooin ower t' chimley ahtsahd.

They've coorted for years an' Ah'm reight glad an' fain
    They've mad up ther mahnds to tee t' knot.
When two young uns love, it's a seet better gain
    To wed an' mak sewer o' ther lot.

There'll be ringin o' bells an' singin' an' stuff,
    An' clatter o' knives, spooins an' forks;
There'll be suppin o' ale an' takkin' o' snuff,
    An' pullin' an' poppin' o' corks.

There'll be kissin' an' cuddlin' an' shakkin' o' hands,
　　There'll happen be two or three tears;
An' maybe, enah, there'll be music fra t' bands,
　　All nations o' laughin an' cheers.

There'll be wahrmin' o' t' hahse, wi' spice-cake an' cheese,
　　An' teein o' t' hoss-shoe o' t' door;
An' happen i' tahm shoo'll bahnce on her knees
　　A barn nivver thowt on afoor.

If ye'll nobbut agree to be pairtners, ye two,
　　Baht fratchin' an' nengin', Ah meean,
Ye'll hev nowt but real happiness all yer life through,
　　An' ye'll live all yer young days ageean.

Wilfrid J Halliday (WR)

The Tyke

It's Ripon for rowels,
　　and Shevvil' for steel,
It's Pudsa for puddings,
　　you knaw varry weel.
At Whitby there's t' abbey
　　where Caedmon once sung,
At Halifax, t' gibbet,
　　where t' bad-uns were hung:
At Ilkla there's t' moors,
　　there's t' Minster at York,
And I've heard of a place
　　where they fratch when they talk.
But for t' marrer to t' fowk —
　　you can choose where you like,
There's nobody so friendly
　　as t' real Yorkshire Tyke.

Wilfrid J Halliday (WR)

An example of the verse of Brenda English of Whitby, who pub-
lished, with her friend Irene Sutcliffe, several excellent booklets of
North Riding dialect.

Mr and Mrs Camster

Mr and Mrs Camster
Oft took a walk bi t' dyke.
For all at they war married,
They warn't a bit alike.

T' war Sunda when Ah met 'em,
Ah shooted oot: 'Good day!'
An' 'e war pleeased ti see me,
Bud t' missis leeaked away.

Then he said: "Warm i' t' sunshine!'
An' pleasant-like he grinned.
Sha fassen'd up 'er jacket
An' muttered: 'Cawd i' t' wind!'

An' if thoo leeaks aboot tha,
Ah lay thoo'll offens finnd
Sum's allus warm i' t'sunshine
An' others cawd i' t' wind.

Brenda English (NR)

Fred Brown (1893–1980) was one of Yorkshire's finest worker-poets.
Born in Keighley, he moved to Huddersfield, working in textile mills
for over half a century. His verse, which appeared over the years in
such journals as the YDS Transactions *and in the anthology of*
fifty of his poems, The Muse Went Weaving, *is original, sometimes*
quirky, often profound — and almost always realistically reflects the
view of workers in the mill-towns.

Loom Harmony

Clickerty-clack, Clackerty-clack,
   Shuttle and bobbin'
Clickerty-clack, clackerty-clack,
   Mary Jane's sobbin';

T' tuner's upbraided her,
  She's forgetten to oil;
Clickerty-clack, clackerty-clack,
  Mullock and moil.

Fred Brown (WR)

The Three Weavers

I saw three weavers, sharing
A common task, and staring;
A penny for a thought,
Here's what three pennies bought.

What do you see, Alice May?
I see a warp of worsted grey.

What do you see, Mary Downs?
I see a weave of drabs, and browns.

What do you see, Ethel Grace?
I see a pattern of blossom and lace.

  Alice May is married;
  Mary Downs is old
  Ethel Grace, she loves a lad
  From Wainwright's Fold.

Fred Brown (WR)

Gi' us Peace

'Is it naah?' whispered t' trees.
'Maybe naah!' murmur'd t' wind.
'Happen naah!' burbled t' stre-am.
An' t' trees—
An' t' wind—
An' t' stre-am

(In a queer wak'nin' dre-am)
Ga' voice to ther thowts
In t' whisperin'.

'Ah'll goah!' said t' wind.
'Aye, goah!' urged t' stre-am.
'Do goah!' begged t' trees.
An' t' quick wind went speedin'
Wheer bairnies ligged bleedin'
Mangled an' riven
Stark-limbed
God-given,
Tip-toss'd childer.

Then foller'd wheer t' blast-guns
(Death's lakins) hed been
And wistfully skenned
I' warrin' men's een.

'Not yet!' groaned t' trees
Foldin' deep into t' neet.
'Not yet!' purled t' stre-am
As it rullied fra' t' seet.

Fred Brown (WR)

Supermarket

A little wire basket —
Tempters on t' shelves —
It cums a bit cheaper
When you help yourselves.

A packet o' biscuits —
A nahce fancy cake —
Fill up yer baskets!
Ther's nooa need to bake.

Line up at t' counter —
They tot up yer score —
Yer've got what yer needed,
An' happen a bit more.

Ah remembered t' owd shop
Wi' its cleean sanded floor —
An' buckets an' brushes
Hung swingin' near t' door.

Yer joined in wi' t' gossip,
An' monny a jooake —
When whiskery old Sam
Tipped yer flaar into t' pooake.

Old Sam hed nooa baskets,
Nooa slick shiny till;
But noa chromium platin'
Could match Samuel's goodwill.

Fred Brown (WR)

Not for Viewing

If there wor winders i' hearts,
An' fan-leets i' mahnds,
What sales there'd be
For curtains an' blahnds!

Fred Brown (WR)

F A Carter, like Fred Brown, spoke the dialect of the Huddersfield area, but many of his poems concern the wide open spaces of the Dales, including this cheery springtime celebration of upper Wharfedale.

Thowts i' Springtime

Come on, tha's surely had enough
O' dowly winter dumps!
It's spring ageean; up-end thissen;
It's tahme tha stirred thi stumps,

Or else tha weean't desarve to see
A lahmestun wall ageean,
Or curlews ower Langstrothdale
Wheer t' air is keen an' cleean.

Aye, keen enough, Ah'll bet it is,
Up amang t' fells an' gills!
T' gre't aat o' dooars — Ah know, Ah know;
'There's cowd i' them theer hills'.
Ay, theer it is, Ah'm gettin on;
Ah can't goo on for ivver
Roamin' abaat on t' tops as if
Ah still were young an' clivver.

Nay, drat it, if Ah haven't gooan
An' set missen agate
Thinkin' o' Oughtersha' an' Cray,
An' watterfalls i' spate!
Ah dooan't know 'at its all that far;
A bus 'ud just do t' trick.
Ah'll 'lift up me een to t' hills' ageean —
Na wheer's me walkin'-stick?

F A Carter

A light-hearted piece of verse, popular as one of Stanley Holloway's monologues, was the following, written by R P Weston and Bert Lee in 1940. They had a range of successes, starting with 'Goobye-ee' in 1917, and including 'Brahn Boots' and 'With her head tucked underneath her arm'. In this poem they manage to give their lines a good Yorkshire flavour. It is complemented by one written for Yorkshire Day 1991, and which has the same mock-boastful approach.

Yorkshire Pudden

Hi waitress, excuse me a minute, now listen,
I'm not finding fault, but here, Miss,
The 'taters' look gradely — the beef is a' reet,
But what kind of pudden is this?

It's what? — Yorkshire pudden! now coom coom coom coom,
It's what! Yorkshire pudden d'ye say?
It's pudden, I'll grant you — it's some sort o' pudden,
But not *Yorkshire* pudden, nay nay!

The real Yorkshire pudden's a poem in batter,
To make one's an art, not a trade;
Now listen to me — for I'm going to tell thee
How t' first Yorkshire pudden wor made.

A young angel on furlough from Heaven
Came flying above Ilkley Moor,
And this angel, poor thing — got cramp in her wing
And coom down at owd woman's door.

The owd woman smiled and said 'Ee, it's an angel,
Well I am surprised to see thee.
I've not seen an angel before but tha'rt welcome,
I'll make thee a nice cup o' tea.'

The angel said 'Ee, thank you kindly, I will.'
Well, she had two or three cups of tea,
Three or four Sally Lunns, and a couple of buns —
Angels eat very lightly, you see …

Then the angel jumped up and said 'Gimme your bowl,
Flour and t' watter and eggs, salt and all,
And I'll show thee how we make puddens in Heaven,
For Peter and Thomas and Paul.'

Then t' owd woman gave her the things, and the angel
Just pushed back her wings and said 'Hush!'
Then she tenderly tickled the mixture wi' t' spoon
Like an artist would paint with his brush …

Aye, she mixed up that pudden with Heavenly magic,
She played with her spoon on that dough
Just like Paderewski would play the piano,
Or Kreisler, now deceased, would twiddle his bow.

And when it wor done and she put it in t' oven,
She said to t' owd woman 'Goodbye'.

Then she flew away, leaving the first Yorkshire pudden
That ever was made — and that's why

It melts in the mouth, like the snow in the sunshine,
As light as a maiden's first kiss;
As soft as the fluff on the breast of a dove,
Not elephant's leather, like this!

It's real Yorkshire pudden that makes Yorkshire lasses
So buxom and broad in the hips.
It's real Yorkshire pudden that makes Yorkshire cricketers
Win county championships ...

R P Weston & Bert Lee

Yorksher Pud

Yorksher Puddin' — that's the stuff!
Us Yorksher lads can't gerr enough
An' t' Yorksher lasses, bless the'r 'earts
From parkin pigs an' apple tarts,
From tripe ter meyt-an'-tatie pie,
The' knaw just 'ah ter satisfy:
Champion cooks 'oo nivver err —
'Ummer to all yond 'cordon bleu'!
Ther' s nowt ter beat a Yorkshire Pud,
Cookin' which is in the'r blood —
Nut summat med bi kitchin trollops,
Served i' sad an' soggy dollops,
Same as dooaf i' thi mahth,
(T' sooart o' tack tha gets i' t' sahth);
No! Gowlden-brahn, beyond compare,
Grand an' crispy, leet as air;
Square or rahnd, it doesn' t matter —
T' secret's elbow-grease i' t' batter,
Wi t' tastiest jeeuices aht o' t' beef,
An' onion gravy's t' aperitif,
Cos if tha wants ter do t' job well

Tha starts wi t' Puddin' by itsel';
Aye. That's traditional Yorksher way,
An' why they allus eeused ter say:
'Them 'at eyts mooast Puddin' gets mooast meyt',
So the'd fill the'r bellies wi all the' could eyt,
An' when t' beef guz rahnd ther's mooare ner the' thowt
Cos t' brussen-guts 'ad room fer next ter nowt!
Oh, it's mooarish, is Yorksher, but real Puddin's rare:
Off-comed-uns try it — bud they 'aven't got t' flair:
It's in t' mixin', an' t' beatin', an' t'owd well-worn tins,
Nut burnt black rahnd t'edges like an offerin' fer sins,
Or undone i' t' middle — nah that *is* a job!
But baked ter perfection ter seeuit ivvery gob ...
It' s an 'eaven-sent secret — it runs in wer blood ...
An' if food's served up yonder — ther'll be Yorksher Pud!

Arnold Kellett (WR)

Ruth Hedger, born in York, and for some time living in Coxwold, where her father was vicar, wrote many lively poems about life in the country, including one portraying the scorn once felt for local lads marrying off-comed-uns *from far-away London.*

London Piece

Ah nivver thowt it 'ud coome ti pass;
Oor Jackie's wedded a city lass!
Wi' poodther an' paint she clarts 'er phiz,
An' she talks lahke fawks on t' wiyerless diz:
Fower years 'e wer' coortin' Robi'son' niece,
Bood 'e's been an' getten a Loondon Piece.

She walks oop t' village on 'eels that 'igh
All t' lartle lads mocks 'er, mincin' by;
'Er sket's that tight she could nivver fraame
Ti climm ower t' stahle; whyah, yer'd think 'er laame.
Till she clicks oop 'er petticawts, bowld as brass —
Yon shaameless Piece of a Loondon lass!

Annie Robi'son's awmly; aye,
Bood 'er ooncle's getten a bit put byah;
She's a 'oose-proud lass, is Robi'son' Annie —
She's quiyet an' menseful, kahnd an' canny;
An' she'll get 'is brass when 'e dees, will t' niece;
Jack's getten nowt wiv 'is Loondon Piece.

She can't baake breead an' she weean't scroob t' flooar,
Nor yet wash t' step on 'er awn froont dooar;
'is Dad wer' allus a careful man,
Bood she's maade Jack buy on t' instalment plan;
'E'll rew', says t' Meeasther, 'Bood t' fond yoong ass
Mun fick it oot, wiv 'is Loondon lass.'

Ruth Hedger (NR)

*Gordon Allen North was born in 1904 at Scholes, near Holmfirth, and
his deep affection for the moors of the South Pennines is seen in the first
of these poems, followed by two more fine poems — short, but sweet.*

Ah'm Comin' Back ...

Ah'm comin back, Ah'm stalled o' t' leets;
    Ah'm sick to deeath o' city streets;
An' t' city's ways Ah's nivver leearn,
    Ah'm coming back to t' hills ageean.
Ah'm comin back, there's nowt else fo't
    Mi belly warks wi this mad lot,
Ah'm comin back to t' wind on t' fells,
    To t' cotton-grass an' t' heather-bells.
Ah'm comin back, mi thost to sleck
    I' t' peeaty wine o' t' Ewden Beck,
Mi heart to wahrm, mi sowl to fill
    Wi' t' seet o' t' stars thro Hartcliff Hill.
Ah'm fain for t' tang o' peeat ageean,
    For t' scent o' t' gorse an' t' ling,
For t' seet o' t' lapwing on her peeak,
    An' t' moorcock, low on t' wing.
Mi heart, it's set i' th' upland ways;

An', reyt daan i' mi booans,
Ah'm one gret wark for th' Heigh Lad Ridge,
   T' Crow Chin, an' t' Glory Stooans.

Gordon Allen North (WR)

Love Song

Keep thi lips for love, lass,
   An' keep thi lips for me;
Share, if tha mun, thi beauty,
   An' t' twinkle i' thi ee,
An' don thissen i' fol-de-rols
   For all the wo'ld to see —
But keep thi lips for love, lass,
   Oh, keep thi lips for me.

Gordon Allen North (WR)

A Lovely Lass is Shoo

Ah took her i' mi airms today,
   A lovely lass is shoo;
Ah kussed her, an' shoo bad me stay
   An' stroke her achin' broo;
Her skin's as snod as glass itsen,
   Her lips are honey-sweet:
Oh, what new wo'lds 'll oppen when
   Shoo's i' mi airms toneet?

Gordon Allen North (WR)

*A memory of a children's Christmas morning in the East Yorkshire
countryside in the days of candle-light and simple presents.*

To my Sister

Dis thoo remember Chrismasses when we were lahtle lasses?
We 'elped oor Mam ti mak mince-pies an then we polished
   t' brasses;
An' then we gor a pie apiece an put oor awn mark on 'em,
An' set em up on t' chimbleypiece for Santa Claus ti ger 'em.

We hung oor stockin's up on t' post at boddom end o t' bed,
And then we thried ti get ti sleep becos me Faather said
'Onny bairn at Santa indthers gets 'er stockin' full o' cindthers!'
When we woke o Chrismas morn we ad nae cannle-leet,
We gor oor stockins offen t' post an' guessed wi' all oor might,
An' then we shooted tiv oor Mam ti let us ev a leet.
She cummed wi t' cannle iv 'er hand, 'er neetgoon lang an' white,
She sat on t' bed an' watched us undeeing of all t' sthrings—
She seemed as foorce as we were wi' all oor lahtle things.
There were pooaks o' choclit pennies, an' sugar-candy pigs,
An' goodies, nuts, an' apples, an' rid-tipped sugar cigs,
An' doon at very boddom, when we thowt we'd gor all t' things,
A lahtle conny box apiece wi two real gowden rings!
An' then we packed 'em up ageean an' thried ti get ti sleep,
Bud Ah kept thinkin o' t'mince-pies, an went ti ev a peep.
Matches Ah fun an' sthruck a leet an' leeaked on t' chimbleyshelf,
T' pies weern't where we'd left 'em, seea, thinks Ah ti me-self,
Ah's sure awd Santa's getten em — as sure as t' dog es fleas! —
Them lads at skeeal was tellin lies — Cos me Dad eats his
    wi cheese!

Claire Ellin (ER)

*This is one of the many delightful little poems by Will Clemence
which once regularly graced the pages of* Dalesman *magazine in
the 'Young Fred' series.*

A Hoss

A hoss is t' nicest thing Ah knaw;
It nivver answers back;
It pulls gurt looads, does a'most owt,
If nobbut yer've got t' knack.

Ah like ter feel one muzzle up
An' let me pat it heead.
Yer'd a'most thowt it thenked me fo'
A little bit o' breead.

Ah offen ride on Oldroyd's mare,
Shoo's big an' strong an' brooad,
An' Ah'm reight prahd o' Bessie when
Shoo clop, clop, clops up t' rooad.

A hoss he's got more sense ner fowk
An' whippin' 'em is mean,
It's t' hoss's feelin's what they hurt
Ah've seen it i' the'r een.

Will Clemence (WR)

The sight of discarded blinnders *('blinkers' used to prevent a horse from seeing sideways) inspires the poet Kathleen Stark to lament the disappearance of horses from the farms.*

T' Hoss Blinnders

Ah seed t' hoss blinnders hung in t' stable theer,
   Dusty an' dowly, same as summat felled;
Nivver i' use Ah s' think these monny years,
   Since tractors come, an' t' hosses all was selled.

Yance, oot at work in t' fields in t' wind an' t' sun
   Warm wi' hoss sweeat, yon brokken bit champed breet
Noo, t' blinnders is but kelterment, worth nowt;
   Wi' tractors here, there's not yah hoss i' seet.

Kathleen Stark

An original and witty comment by Keighley poet and local histori-an Ian Dewhirst, on the fact that woolcombers used to share a heat-ed pot in which they put their combs to keep them warm. This chap, not fond of company, had his own pot, and was therefore a pot o' one.

Pot o' One

From t' varry day mi life begun
Ah've allus bin a pot o' one,
An' up till t' time 'at it mun end
Ah didn't think 'at Ah sud mend.

Sin' fust Ah left mi babby-pen
Ah've bin ovver-mindful o' missen:
Ther's nawther care ner choice ner fun,
No sharin', for a pot o' one.

But oh, dear lass, tha's ta'en mi heart
An' shocked mi little warld apart,
An' pot o' one's no use to me
Now Ah'm so much in love wi' thee!

Ah can't abide thee aht o' seet,
On pins abaht thee, day an' neet;
Ther's nobbut one thing we can do:
Lass, sal we be a pot o' two?

An' if it pleases t' Lord above,
Through joy an' sympathy an' love,
I' time together, thee an' me,
We's happen mak' a pot o' three.

Ian Dewhirst (WR)

Arthur Jarratt was a popular writer of East Riding dialect, and though an accountant working in Hull, he so identified with the life of country-folk — and especially Methodist chapel-folk — that, the words of Bill Cowley, 'in every verse are natural phrases of vivid dialect'. His poems are favourites for public reading, especially at the York 'Christmas Crack' of the Yorkshire Dialect Society, including 'The Innkeeper', read by a real East Yorkshire countryman, Irwin Bielby of Pocklington.

Lang Sarmons

Whenivver sarmon's ower lang — an' some are to be sure —
It allus thinks me on aboot a spot called Botton Moor.
We ed a lahtle Bethil theer: it was a bonny plaace,
Ah offens used ti wend mi way ti seek oot Thrawn o Graace.

An' preeachers used ti cum tiv it, an'mah wod, sum was queer!
Noo this consarns awd Peter Land: he'd cummed for monny
    a year.

He warn't si bad as preeachers go — his lungs were rare an' sthrang!
Throuble with awd Peter was — he lasted ower lang!

Ah nivver took a deeal o nooat a sooart o check ti keeap.
Ah nivver took mich nooatice cos Ah allus went ti sleeap.
Bud if ye reckoned up at all, Ah'll warrant ye'd be safe
If ye said his shortest sarmon was an'oor an'a 'afe.

Noo, Ah leeaked efther chapil, an' steward, he was Ben;
An' we ed oor stock ti fodder, we was nobbut labrin' men.
An' sooa, when Ben he sez ti me: 'It's Peter Land next Sunda,'
Sez Ah: 'If summat isn't done, he'll ev us theer whahl Munda.'

Sez Ben: 'It's nobbut waste o tahm ti ax him ti be short,
We'll etti tak sum other rooad — noo, can ye think of aught?'
'Why ay,' Ah sez: 'Ah can an' all; Ah sud a thowt afoor.
If Ah can onny worrk it, we'll be lowsed insahd an oor.'

'Ah allus fills them chapil lamps ti top wi parafeen.
Next Sunda though, Ah deean't knaw as Ahs'll be si keen.
Ah'll mak it sooas them lamps'll fizzle oot at seven o'clock!
Ah rackon that'll give awd Peter Land a bonny shock!'

Sooa, when next Sunda cummed along, yon lamps was
      ommost dhry.
Ah's think the' hardlins oil eneeaf ti dhroon a lahtle fly.
Ah sez ti Ben: 'Ah onny ooaps we git collection taen.'
'Well, if we deean't,' sez Ben: 'Ah reckon fooaks'll cum again.'

Well, up cums Peter iv his thrap, an' maks a goodish start;
An' efther afe an' oor we was well through fommost part.
So Ben teks up collection, an awd man puts on his specs.
An' fun his place i' Exodus, and fezzoned on is tex.

It was summat aboot Mawses — an' we'd eeard it oft afoor —
An' then Ah noaticed somehoo leet was lewkin' middlin poor.
Ah leeaned across ti Ben, an' sez, when Peter starts ti spoot:
'Ah wunder wheer'll be Mawses when these chapil leets gan oot?'

It wasn't lang afoor fooaks was wunderin' what was matther.
An' poor awd man, he'd scarcelins getten Mawses oot o' watther,
When yan o' lamps starts fickin, an' it varry seean gans oot.
Ah'd been a thrifle ower keen i' thrimmin that, Ah doot.

There was afe a dozen lamps i' spot, an' fost yan, then another
Went blobbin oot, an' fooaks began ti get intiv a smother;
Till nobbut yan was left aleet, an' it nigh pulpit rail.
Thinks Ah: 'It weeant be lang noo afoor it begins ti fail.'

An' Peter kep on preeachin — he nooaticed nowt was wrang:
He was reeadin frev his paper, an' it kep im ower tthrang ...
Bud that pulpit lamp kep bonnin as though it'd last all neet.
Ah deean't recall Ah've ivver knawn a lamp that bonnt si breet!

It'd brek mi art ti tell ye ivvrything that we'd ti bahd.
An' that dhratted lamp was bonnin efther fooaks'd got ootsahd.
We'd nivver been si late afoor — just wantin afe past nahn!
Sez Ben: 'Thoo gits thi oil frev a better spot than mahn!'

At supper tahm, ma missus sez: 'Yon lamps was rare'n dhry!
Ah appened leeak at pulpit, so Ah filled it varry nigh' ...
An' next day, Ben, he sez ti me: 'We'll thrim them lamps ni moor.
We'll etti just put clock on, like we've allus done afoor!'

Arthur Jarratt (ER)

The Innkeeper

Breekfast? Why lass, Ah's nut ungery,
Ah nivver thowt on for ti eeat,
An' Ah's breet as a bullace this mornin,
When Ah owt ti be deead o' mi feeat!

Last neet — there'll be nivver nowt like it,
If Ah live tiv a hundhred an' ten.
Ah've bin chaanged owerneet somehoo, Mary,
An' Ah's capped hoo it happened, an' when.

Thoo'll recall that young couple fra Nazareth:
We'd nowheer ti put 'em i' inn:
Well, Ah fun 'em a plaace doon i' coo-shade
— Bud weather was desperate thin:

Sooa, when Ah'd all visitors sattled,
An' thoo hard asleep i' thi bed,
Ah lowsened awd Jess frev her kennel,
An' wended mi way doon ti shed.

It was clearer nor dayleet i' fowdyard:
Ommost midneet it was — moon at full.
Nut a glimmer frid hooses i' village,
An' snaw covered grund, soft as wool.

They'd ed nowt ti eeat ti ma knowledge,
So Ah browt 'em a bite an' a sup,
An' some oil i' case lamp wanted thrimmin,
An' happins, to lap bairn up.

Then Ah tended ti coos, an' ti Jenny,
— An' Ah've nivver knawn cattle si calm,
An' Ah browt some cleean sthraw doon for manger,
Just ti mak seear at bairn was wahrm.

Ah deean't think they nooaticed me scarcelins,
As Ah rawmed aboot sidin' spot through.
They wor taen up wi lewkin' at bairn
— An' it mother es same name as thoo!

Sike a wee, conny thing it was, Mary,
Poor bairn! Ommost lost amang sthraw!
… But Ah couldn't distorrb 'em mich langer,
So Ah left 'em an' stood oot i' snaw.

A still neet it was — sthraange an quiet,
As Ah leeaned up agen dooar jamb …
Then Ah fancied Ah heeard soond o' music,
As thaw stars was all singin a psalm!

At fosst — well, Ah thowt Ah was dhreeamin':
But they'd heeard it at pinfowd an' all,

An Ah seed 'em come runnin doon hillsahde,
An makkin their way sthraight ti stall!

It was Rewben, and Shep, and young Davy,
They'd bin up at top tentin sheeap.
They wor towld ti come doon inti village,
Wheer they'd finnd lartle bairn asleeap.

Noo, sthrangest of all was awd Rewben:
Leeavin lambs nobbut yistidda born!
But all he would say when Ah axed him —
'The Lord'll tak care of his awn!'

Well, summat was dhrawin me, Mary.
So Ah went in wi Rewb an' his men.
We stood a bit lewkin' at bairn ...
But Ah hardlins knaw what happened then.

We went doon on oor knees theer i' staable,
Awahle mother took bairn ov her knee,
An' she crooned a soft lullaby ower it,
Tahme we knelt: Rewben, Shep, Dave, an' me.

Noo, God's bairns is all on 'em lovely,
 — Why oor awn was a bonny, wee thing.
An' Ah play wiv em, noss em, an love 'em —
Yit we knelt like we would tiv a king!

Sooa that's why Ah's nut varry ungery:
Ah'd like ti walk hills all day lang.
 — Bud we've visitors' vittles ti see tiv,
Varry seean we'll be booath on us thrang.

But fosst, walk wi' me doon ti coo-shade:
Ah feel some day, when we've getten awd,
We'll be glad we leeaked efther that bairn,
An' fun it a plaace oot o' caud.

Arthur Jarratt (ER)

Bill Cowley (see page 27) farmed for over forty years at Potto Hill,
and in his Cleveland Anthology *included this tribute to his uncle,*
Charlie Coates of Welbury, who died in 1951.

Epitaph for a Countryman

Thoo's warked for lang eneeaf — noo bide i' peace
I' t' chotch-garth 'ere, bi t' fields thoo kept si weel;
Cum spring, thi coos an' cauves 'll graze nigh-and,
An' t' soil thoo luved, i' sleep 'll be thi seal.

I' field an' forest noo for fifty yeear
Neea yan cud stack or theeak or fell a tree,
Snig, slash, maw, milk, drahve 'osses or guide t' pleeaf,
Dig drains or lig a hedge as weel as thee.

Lang sin thoo bowled for t' village creckit team,
Knocked runs, scored goals, wan monny a runnin' prize;
Life's innins ower'd noo, rist quiet a whahl
They'll likelins need thy help i' Paradise!

Bill Cowley (NR)

One of the many nostalgic poems written by Harry Brooks about
his native Queensbury, between Bradford and Halifax. The first few
lines will be incomprehensible to most readers without recourse to the
glossary — but this is a vivid picture of life in the good/bad old days.

T' Navvy 'Ahses

Winter-'edge, voider an' set-pot,
Posser an' sycamoor prop,
Piggin an' pitcher an' possnit,
Breead-fleyk an' 'arston an' mop,
Caw-rake an' fire-point an' ass-nook,
'Avverbreead, paarkin an' dooaf,
Frummerty, thick-seeam an' pestil,

Possit, mulled ale an' spice-looaf,
Stee-'oile an' cham'er an' nessy,
Garrit, slop-kitchin, stooane sink,
Cellar-'eead, cornish an' troughin' —
All theease owd words mak' mi think
O' t' owd days when wi wer childer
Livin' i' t' owd back-ter-backs
T' local fowk called t' Navvy 'Ahses —
Like the' wor nobbut owd shacks.
But the' wor 'ooamly an' cawsy,
All built o' Queensbury stooane,
When the' browt t' Gurt Northern Railway
Wheeare, afooare then, the' wor nooan …
Up t' top o' t' streets wor t' stooan nessies,
Stooan flags o' t' roofs an' nooa frills;
White-scrubbed wood seeats wi' rahnd lids on,
T' walls lime-weshed twice ivvry year,
Squares o' newspaper o' t' dooar nail,
(Summat ter read, cahrin' theear).
Then awf-way dahn ther' wor t' ginnils,
Leeadin' through inter t' next street,
T' fowk each side awned oo wor commin'
As the'r clogs clomped through at neet.
All t' ahses 'ed the'r awn cellars,
Stooane steps ter t' owd cellar'eead,
T' kitchin an' t' 'ahseplace wor stooan-flagged
An' stooan steps twisted an' reared
Up rahnd a corner ter t' cham'ers,
Then cawm another steeap stee,
A wood 'un this time, up ter t' garrit.
Through t' shut i' t' roof we could see
T' stars twinklin' dahn as we ligged theeare,
I' t' iron bed, cawsy an' snug,
An' we stepped aht when we wakkened
On tiv a gurt sheepskin rug;
Tabbed 'uns wor o' t' flooar i' t' ahseplace,
Gooatskins o' t' backs o' t' armcheers,
An' t' lang-case clock i' t' far corner

Knacked as it 'ed done for years.
T' range wor blackleeaded an' shinin',
T' kettle a-singin' on t' 'ob,
Ivvrythin' dusted an' polished,
All on us tiv us awn job.
Wark wor nooan eeasy ter come by,
T brass 'ed ter gooa a lang way,
But fowk all 'elped wun another
Mooare ner what some do ter-day.
But it's gooid mem'ries we cleave tul —
If we'd ter tell t' trewth, chewse 'ah,
Rough an' smooth ta'en all together,
'Appen we'd rayther live nah!

Harry Brooks (WR)

Written in 1960 when there were still plenty of working coalmines in South Yorkshire, and the quiet on the surface belied the hard graft deep underground.

On t' Surface

Days, afters,
Through the neet,
Ther's a seathin' quiet
Along t' main street.

T' mornin' steams,
T' pit-head monster simmers,
As it gulps t' pit-men
Like a lion its dinners.

It's nivver 'Good mornin',
But 'All reight, Bill?'
'Sam!' 'Nah, Jim',
'Okay, Will?'

Or else t' silent nod,
That's t' usual greeatin':

The' goa abaht ther business,
Noa fussin' wi' meeatin'.

Ther's a steady throb;
T' noise from t' coil-lurries,
T' owd ten-past t' hour,
But nob'dy 'urries.

T' pit-buzzer mooans,
T' tractors shatter,
Milkdrays drooan,
'eead-scarved women natter.

But all this is rare,
An explosion i' t' calm.
It lasts for one minute,
Then quietens dahn.

Nigel Leary (WR)

*One of the light pieces of verse written by Sydney Martin of York, play-
ing on the Yorkshireman's advice to his son to keep his own counsel.*

Knaw Nowt

Yan o' t' sayings of old wad be
'Knaw nowt, mi lad, knaw nowt.
Whativver question thoo gits axed,
Knaw nowt, mi lad, knaw nowt.'

When his lad went off ti skeeal
An' browt yam his repoort,
Fayther seeamed a bit upset
An' sent skeeal boss a nooat.

'Thoo's nut deean ower weeal' said Dad,
'Nut as weeal as Ah'd a thowt.'
Seea t' lad replied 'Thoo allus said
"Knaw nowt, mi lad, knaw nowt!"'

Sydney Martin (ER)

Michael Park, secretary of the Yorkshire Dialect Society, writes in the dialect of the Scarborough area about bletherskites *(gossips).*

Bletherskites

Ah hev two timepieces,
An nawther on 'em match,
Yan's a girt alarum clock,
T' ither's a lahtle watch.

T' alarum clock varies wildly,
Bud t' bell rings lood an fine,
T' wristwatch ligs theer quiet,
Bud it keeaps perfect tahm.

T' world hes monny talkers,
An' quiet fooaks thoo'll meet,
Bud, him at shoots oot loodest
Is rarely t' yan that's reet!

Michael Park (NR)

One of the many poems written and presented on stage by Geoffrey Robinson who, under the pen-name of 'Owd Joss', wrote a humorous dialect column for the Hull papers in the 1970s and '80s.

Nut Let On

Yah yeear when Tom 'n' me was bairns
'n' it cem ti Kessmass Eeave,
Wa cudn't get ti sleeap at ahll,
As weel ya maht beleeave.

I' bed wa talked aboot nex' daay
'n' ahll wa shaaped ti deea;
Wa'd 'ev a reet good tahm 'n' ahll,
O' that, ther waan't mich feear.

Then wa 'eeard oor Mam 'n' Dad i' t' stairs,
Then feeat-steps pitter-pattrin'.
'Pretend ti be asleeap', Ah ses.
'The'v cum ti stop us chatt'rin.'

Thru t' bedroom door the tip-tooaed in,
Oor ees suppooasedly shut,
Then inti t' piller-caase 'ung oot
Sum grandish things the' put.

Wa tak oor toys 'n' gaames doon-stairs
Next morn, as chuff as owt;
'Wha, Dad, noo leeak at them', says Mam,
'Wat Santa Klaws 'es browt.'

It pleeased 'em weel ti nut let on,
Sooa we gev nowt awaay,
'n' ther's neea doot ahll on us 'ed
A ''Appy Kessmass Daay!'

Geoffrey Robinson (ER)

*Farming with her husband in the northernmost part of Yorkshire,
Ruth Harrison Dent, for many years a key worker in the Yorkshire
Dialect Society, has had many of her poems published, including
this cameo of a mother's anxiety.*

Skeul

Wi' satchel on her back, she gans
Away doon t' laane te t' gate
Tis fost day off ti skeul, tha knaas,
I hooape she weean't bi late.

'Tis lonely Ah'll bi when she's gone,
Ah's nut afeeard ti say
An Ah'll bi watchin' tahm cum roond
Ti fower o'clock teday

Hoo will she git on wi' her sums?
Ah wunner if t' milk's pure?
These thowts cum tummlin' ti mi mahnd,
Aye, these an' monny mooare.

Ah wunner if she'll lahke all t' food?
An' wesh her hands i' t' breeaks?
An' wheeall bi theeare ti pick her up
If she a tummel teeaks?

Mi lahtle lassie's gan, tha knaas,
She's oot o' mah control,
An' other influences ther'll be
Ower body, mahnd, an' sowl.

Eh noo, Ah musn't think lahke this,
An' git intiv a stife,
T'owd sayin' tells me, 'Skeul days is
Best days o' all thi life'.

Ruth Harrison Dent (NR)

This little poem highlights the fact that some of the best speakers of dialect are very different in appearance from the traditional image of Yorkshire folk.

Diff'runt

Ah wor born an' bred i' Bratford
An' Ah'm prahd o' bein' a Tyke —
But Ah'm not like other Yorksher fowk,
Ah'm sort o' diffrunt, like.

Oh Ah'm partial t' Yorksher bitter
An' Ah luv mi Yorksher pud,
An' Ah'd feight like 'ell t' lick Lancasher
As onny on us would.

But still fowk say Ah'm diffrunt,
That ther's summat not quite reight,
Almost as if their 'earin' wer
At odds wi' what's i' sight.

But Ah say Ah'm a Yorksherman,
In spite o' what fowk say,
Tho mi muther comes from Delhi
An' mi faither from Bombay.

Derek Lupton (WR)

Like Robert Burns, the poet F W Hirst addresses a mouse, this one in the miner's coal-pit, about to be closed down.

A Deep Grave

Little mahse, wotivver a' ta dooin' dahn 'eeare i' t' pit?
The've neearly all gone nah ... tha'll be on thi awn in a bit;
Sooin' tha weeant be able ter fill thissen wi' fat an' bread,
Ner rive up all t' snap papers ter mak thissen a little bed.

Ah ta listenin' ter me? The're cloisin' this pit fer good;
If tha aren't payin' nooa 'eed, tha surely should:
In a day or two the'll be chuckin' nooa mooare snap away;
An' ther'll be nowt for thi t' eyt at t' end o' t' day.

Ah can see thi sittin' theeare — tha doesn't seem ter care;
T' thowt o' wot's bahn ter 'appen ter thee, Ah cannot bear...
Ah sahn't be comin' dahn nooa moore after termorrer,
But t' thowt o' thi bein' left dahn 'ere fills me up wi' sorrer.

F W Hirst (WR)

To round off this section, here are three samples of the compiler's own verse, the first a memory of his Wibsey childhood, and the final one having been read on radio one memorable Christmas by Wilfred Pickles.

Back-Street Ballad

Ah wish Ah wor a lad ageean:
By gum! Ah'd mak it crack!
Ah'd laik as long as it wor leet,
An' come 'ooame mucky-black.

Ah'd nivver waste a minute on 't,
Ah'd be in t' street all t' day,
Cos me an' t' lads wi'd nooan bi stuck
Fer summat fresh ter play.

Wi'd 'appen bi Red Indians,
Or gangsters feytin' t' p'lice,
Wi' watter-pistols, dustbin-lids,
An' a gun an' caps apiece.

Wi' gangs an' dens an' bogie-rides
Us lads wer' nivver stalled;
Bud t' mothers said: 'Na then! Think on!
Just come in when tha's called!'

Aye. In them grand short-trahsered days
Wi'd 'appiness galooare …
By Gow! Ter be a lad ageean!
Ah couldn't ask fer mooare!

Arnold Kellett (WR)

A Bit of a Change

A grand Christmas dinner wor sided at last —
Then they all started fratchin' away
Ovver t' programmes they wanted on t' telly —
It wor ruinin' wer Christmas Day.

Some wanted one thing, an' some wanted t'other:
Young uns says, 'We'll 'ave James Bond!'
'An'll nut stand fer that!', Granfatther says —
An' 'e likes 'is awn way, does yond.

'Well sit thissen dahn, then,' Granmother bawls,
'Cahr quiet, an' just clooase thi een!'
So, queer as Dick's 'atband, they all gathered rahnd,
Gawpin' all gawmless at t' screen.

The' switched t' blamed set on … but nowt 'appened—
The'd watch owt nah, on that they agreed,
But choose 'ah the' brayed it an' pawsed it abaht
It wor plain 'at yon telly 'ad deed.

It wor like a bereavement in t' family, tha knaws;
Ivvery face wore a reight solemn frahn —
A gatherin' o' mawks i' daft comic 'ats —
'Eart-sluffened, 'cos t' telly'd brok dahn.

Well, wi lit a grand fire, wi' gurt blazin' logs,
Turned wer backs on t' blank, sackless screen,
An' wi switched on t' wireless at three o'clock,
An' just sat theeare an' listened ter t' Queen.

Then wi all laiked at cards — an' liked it, an' all —
It wor summat we'd nut done fer years —
An' wi supped, an' wi kalled, rahnd yond fire —
Ah felt just like shahtin' three cheers!

Then wi sang a feew carols, an' talked of owld times,
An' passed rahnd all t' nuts, dates an' chocs —
We got on that well, it left us fair capped —
An' we'd all brokken loose from yon box!

A bogie, or home-made children's go-kart.

Tell thee t' treeuth it wor t' best Christmas ivver;
Good company allus ameeuses —
An owld-fashioned Yuletide, baht telly —
Ee … Ah'm reight glad Ah rived aht yon feeuses!

Arnold Kellett (WR)

Yorkshire Christmas

Christmas in t' farm 'ouse
All fettled and clean:
Ther's a feast on yon table
'At's fit for a queen:
A gurt buxom turkey,
Wi' t' trimmins ter come,
An' a champion puddin',
An' sauce laced wi' rum;
Aye, ther's cheese, an' ther's spice-cake
An' summat ter sup —
By gum, lad, tha'll bust
If tha doesn't give up!

Christmas in t' mistal,
All shabby an' bare,
All stinkin' wi cow-muck —
An' t' cattle just stare,
As much as ter say:
'Ther's nowt 'ere fer thee!'
But ovver in t' corner …
Na *then* — dosta see?
Ther's a lass wi' 'er babby,
All snuggled in t' 'ay —
Yon grand little Jesus
On t' fust Christmas Day!

Arnold Kellett (WR)

Yorkshire dialect prose

One of the earliest examples of spoken dialect being recorded is the language of the old servant Joseph in Wuthering Heights *(1847). Emily Brontë based this character, whom she called 'a vinegar-faced hypocrite', on an extreme Calvinist who prided himself on being one of the chosen few whom God has 'picked aht from t' rubbish' of unsaved sinners. Emily here accurately conveys the Howarth speech she has heard all round her — but in later editions her sister Charlotte softened the dialect to make it easier to read, changing words like* dahn *to 'down' and* mooin *to 'moon', for example. What follows is a compilation from the original of various separate utterances by Joseph.*

'T' maisters dahn i' t' fowld. Goa rahnd by t' end ut' laith, if yah went tuh spake tull him.'

'They's nobbut t' missis; and shoo'll nut oppen 't, an (if) ye mak yer flaysome dins till neeght.'

'Aw woonder hagh yah can faishion tuh stand thear i' idleness un wahr, when all on 'em's goan aght! Bud yah're a nowt, and it's noa use talking — yah'll niver mend uh yer ill ways; bud, goa raight tuh t' divil, like yer mother afore ye!'

'T' maister nobbut just buried, and Sabbath nut oe'red, and t' sahnd uh t' gospel still i' yer lugs, and yah dare be laiking! Shame on ye! Sit ye dahn, ill childer! They's good books eneugh if ye'll read 'em; sit ye dahn and think uh yer sowls!'

'Maister Hindley! ... Maister, coom hither! Miss Cathy's riven t' back off "T' Helmet uh Salvation", un' Heathcliff's pawsed his fit intuh t' first part uh "T' Brooad Way to Destruction!" It's fair flaysome ut yah let 'em goa on this gait. Ech! th'owd man ud uh laced 'em properly — bud he's goan!'

'Yon lad gets wahr un wahr! ... He's left th' yate ut t' full swing, un miss's pony has trodden dahn two rigs uh corn, un plottered through, raight o'er intuh t' meadow! Hahsomdiver, t' maister 'ull play t' divil to-morn, and he'll do weel.'

'Aw sud more likker look for t' horse ... It 'ud be tuh more sense. Bud, Aw can look for norther horse, nur man uf a neeght loike this — as black as t' chimbley! und Heathcliff's noan t' chap tuh coom ut maw whistle — happen he'll be less hard uh hearing wi ye!'

'Nay, nay, he's noan at Gimmerton! ... Aw's nivver wonder, bud he's at t' bothom uf a bog-hoile. This visitation worn't for nowt, und Aw wod hev ye tuh look aht, Miss, yah mud be t' next. Thank Hivin for all! All warks togither for gooid tuh them as is chozzen, and picked aht froo th' rubbidge! Tha knaws whet t' Scripture says —'

'Running after t' lads, as usuald! ... It's bonny behaviour, lurking amang t' fields after twelve ut' neeght, wi that fahl, flaysome divil uf a gipsy, Heathcliff! They think Aw'm blinnd; but Aw'm noan, nowt ut t' soart! Aw seed young Linton, boath coming and going, and Aw seed yah ... Yah gooid fur nowt, slattenly witch! Nip up und bolt intuh t' hahs, t' minute yah heard t' maister's horse fit clatter up t' rooad!'

Emily Brontë

A story from the East Riding, old when it was written down by M F C Morris in his Yorkshire Folk Talk *(1892), is perhaps the earliest example of the 'Tom and Jerry' theme.*

T' Moos i' t' Vat

Ther wer yance a moos 'at had gitten it hoal just agaan a greeat vat iv a briewery. T' vat were full o' liquor iv a gen'ral waay, an' yah day t' lahtle moos chanced ti tumm'l in, an' were leyke ti be dhroonded.

'An' seea', says t' moos tiv itsen, 'What mun Ah deea? T' sahds is seea slaap an' brant Ah doot Ah sa'll nivver git yam na mair; Ah's flaayed Ah sa'll 'a' ti gan roond an' roond whahl Ah's dhroonded.'

Bud eftther a bit t' cat pops it heead ower t' top o' t' vat, an' sha leeaks at t' moos an' says, 'What wilt tha gie ma if Ah git tha oot o't' vat?'

Top Withens — inspiration for Wuthering Heights?

'Whya,' says t' moos, 'thoo s'all 'a' ma.'

'Varry weel,' says t' cat, an' seea sha hings hersen doon o' t' insahd; t' moos varry seean ran up t' cat back and lowp'd reet fra t' top o' t' vat intiv it hooal, an' t' cat eftther it.

Bud t' moos were ower sharp an' gat fo'st ti t' hooal, an' then to'ns roond an starts ti laff at t' cat. T' cat wer ommost wahld at that, an' shoots oot, 'Did'nt thoo saay 'at if Ah gat tha oot o' t' vat Ah sud 'a' tha?'

'Aw,' says t' moos, 'Aw', shoo says, 'Bud fowks'll saay owt when the're i' dhrink!'

The following is from a fat note-book of cuttings, an heirloom from my grandmother, who was an avid collector of the writings of John Hartley (see page 48). These appeared in both his Clock Almanack *and various volumes, some serialised in the papers. This extract is from the beginning of* T' Seets i' Lundun, *which had first been published in 1876, an account of Hartley's visit written for his wife Mally in Halifax.*

Sammywell Grimes i' Lundun

A Yorksherman i' Lundun is considered by a gooid monny to be as mich aht o' place as a bull in a china shop (Aw've oft

There's nowt so queer as fowk.

wondered whose bull that wor), but Aw finnd t' fowk 'at hold that nooation know varry little abaat Yorkshermen or else varry little abaat Lundun, for ther's nooa place where its easier to settle daan an' feel at hooam, an' Aw'm sure a Yorksherman can mak hissen at hooam onnywheeare if onnybody can.

When Aw coom to this big an' bustling place, Aw wor capped to finnd fowk here 'at knew nooa mooar abaat us nor we know abaat them. The'd all heeard tell o' Yorksher puddin, Yorksher relish, Yorksher hams, an Yorksher bites; but some on 'em could hardly believe Aw wor a complete Yorksherman, becos Aw hadn't a horse in a helter. Aw met wi' some 'at tried to twit me a bit, an' Aw dare say the' thowt thersen varry cliver; but whether it wor t' size o' mi neive or t' thickness o' mi shoe-soil 'at prevented 'em sayin mich, Aw cannot tell, but the' smiled, an' passed on, an' behaved thersen quite as weel as ye could expect fowk to do 'at's been browt up sich a long way off.

When Aw landed at King's Cross Station theer wor a bit o' bustle, but net hawf as mich noise an' thrustin' as ther is at t' Lankysher and Yorksher of a Setterda' neet; sooa Aw walked aht to have a look raand, an' t' fust thing Aw saw wor a big clock in a steeple, an' thinks 'Aw, that's St. Paul's', but bethinkin' me at all t' pictures Aw'd ivver seen on it had a top like a gurt beehive, Aw thowt Aw'd ax a policeman.

'What do yo call that, maister?'

'It's a quarter past five,' he said.

'Aw can seea that, lump'eead, but Aw want to knaw what the' call t' place?'

'That's the Midland Railway Station'.

'Oh, aye! Why it's ommost as hansum as ahr Taan Hall. But can ta tell me wheeare a chap lives 'at they call John Jones Smith?'

'Nay,' he said, 'I don't think I can. Does he live about here?'

'Why, tha needn't think Aw should ax thee, if he wer living at Bowling or Pudsey. He lives somewheeare abaat here, an' he's what ye call a retired gentleman. He saved a bit o' brass wi' woolsooartin', an' his wife kept a cadger's shop, an' sooa they've come here to live five or six year sin. Yo'll be sure to knaw him — he's rather pockmarked, an' he squints a bit.'

'What street does he live in?'

'Nay, Aw can'tell. All Aw know is, he lives in Lundun, an' 'at he's a bit o' brass. Aw thowt onnybody 'd know him.'

He laff'd, an' walked up to a lot o' cab chaps, an' Aw could tell he wor talkin abaat me bi th' way he yarked his 'eead, an the' stared at me an laffd while the' ommost choaked. Nah, Aw've nowt ageean onnnybody enjoyin' thersen, an' the' wor welcome to laff as mich as they liked if Aw could nobbut finnd Smith, but as Aw could mak nooa sense of a lot o' grinnin geese like them, aw wor just turnin' away away when Aw felt a hand o' mi shoulder an sum'dy said, 'Mr Grimes, I believe.' Aw turned raand, an' Aw should hardly ha believed mi own een if it hadn't been for his. But a chap 'at squints is easy to own, an Aw saw at once 'at it wor the varry identical John Jones Smith 'at Aw'd been axin' abaat, an he'd comed to meet me.

Well, after shakkin hands two or three times, he said he wor glad to see me, an' Aw'm sewer Aw wor glad to see him; an' he said he thowt Aw should do wi a drop o' summat after mi ride. That convinced me 'at he hadn't lost his natteral feelin's, an' 'at t' same heart wor beeatin' under his white shirt as used to beeat under his checker brat when Awd seen him years afooare.

As sooin' as we'd swallered a pint o' fourp'ny, he said, 'Let us make haste to catch the next train.'

'Nay, lad,' Aw said, 'Aw'm nooan gooin' back bi nah; Aw've come to stop a bit, an' Awd rather gooa to yore haase t' fust thing.'

'That's where we are going, but we shall have to ride; it's too far to walk.'

'Nay, net it! It's nooan too far fer me! Aw've walked to Peel Park an' back of a Sunday mornin' monny a time, an' thowt nowt on it.'

'That may be, Mr Grimes, but now you are in London you must allow me to act as guide, and I'll do all I can to show you as much as possible during your stay' ...

We hadn't gooan far when we coom to a station, an' he bowt two tickets, an' we went daan a lot o' steps, an' he said, 'This is the underground railway.'

'Well, if it's reight to yo it's reight to me, tho Aw nivver intended to be put under graand till after Aw wor deead. But

Aw suppooase we shall come up ageean all safe; an if net, awr Mally can draw ten paand off t'club. But Aw say, Smith, does ta think that box o' mine 'll be all reight?'

'What box?'

'Why tha doesn't think aw've come ter Lundun wi mi fingers i' mi maath, does ta? Aw put a box on t' train at Bradford ommost as big as a shut-up bed; an ther's as mich bacon and bacca as 'll fit us booath all t' time Aw stop... Oh, yer needn't hurry, for it's mi name on. It'll nooan be lost, for a mate o' mine painted t' Yorkshireman's coit-of-arms on it, an' he said if onny Lunduner saw that Flea-an'-a-fly-an'-a-flitch-o'-bacon, they'd nooan mell on it.'

John Hartley (WR)

An account of the weekly routine in working-class homes before the First World War written for the YDS Summer Bulletin by the compiler's father, a natural speaker of rich West Riding dialect.

Wick in an' Wick aht

By gum! Ah'd summat on when Ah wor a lad! After mi muther deed Ah wor browt up bi two maiden ants. T' younger on 'em wor called Marth' Ann. She wor a weyver, an' she shahted a lot. I' them days weyvers allus seemed to shaht. Ah suppose it wor wi bawlin ower t' top o' t' loom to ther beam mate, or across t' alley to ther elbow-mate. T' owdest ant wor called Sar' Ann, an' she stopped at 'ooame an' did t' ahse work while Ah went to ter schooil. She wor a tarter, an' all. Talk abaht strict! Ivverything 'ad to be done same as if it wor bi an act o' Parlyment ...

Munda (Wesh Day). There wor allus a bit of a fratch of a Munda mornin. We'd ter ger aht o' bed an ahr sooiner, an' ger all t' weshin' tackle ready afooare ther wor owt t' eyt. It wor my job to leet t' set pot, fill it wi' watter, an' then lig t' thible on t' top so it wornt to seek when Aunt Sar' Ann wanted to stir t' weshin. After this Ah'd ter put t' piggin back under t' sink an bring t' posser an' t' voider aht.

When Ah come 'ooame for mi dinner t' place 'ud bi full o' steeam, an' as sooin as Ah oppened t' door Aunt Sar' Ann 'ould shaht aht: 'Nah, doff thi coit lad, an' come an' twind t' wringer.'

It took some twindin' did yon mengle. It did that! While Ah struggled away Ant Sar' Ann 'ould shove clooathes through, an' when she'd done slahtin abaht we'd sit dahn to wer dinner.

A typical sight in a West Riding house on washday Monday: the set pot, *with a* piggin *or lading can, and a* voider *full of washing.*

On a Munda it wor allus cowd meyt an' pickled onions. An' Ah remember 'at yon onions ewsed to give Ant Sar' Ann a lot o' wind. She nivver said: 'Excuse me', same as they do today. She just said: 'Drat them there onions! Ah weeant ev ony mooare!' But she allus did.

When Ah come back from schooil at teea-time she'd still be agate wi t' weshin'. Ah 'ed to side some o' t' tackle, roll t' carpet back, an' mop t' stooane floor. Then Ah'd dash off to t' paper-shop at t' corner an' liver mi evenin' papers. Ah got awf a crahn a week for it — which wor nooan so bad, for a lad o' twelve.

When Ah 'ad mi teea ther seeamed to be weshin' all ovver t' shop. Ah couldn't see t' fire for t' gurt big clooathes-'oss, an 'ther wor clooathes lines across t' 'arth decked wi shirts an' pants, an' women's stuff, all 'anging dahn from t' breead-fleg.

Tuesda (Ironin' Day). Ah'd an 'ahr longer i' bed, an' Ah'd get up abaht awf past seven. Wi lived in a back-ter-back, tha knaws, an t' closit were dahn t' yard. It wor a cowd do i' winter, Ah'll tell thi.

On a Tuesda ther wor allus kippers for teea, an then t' ironin' 'ould start. It wor a big job, wi t' table cleared, an a two-a-thri flat-irons on t' go. Ah wor glad to gerr aht an laik wi' t' lads, bud when Ah got back at t' supper-time, it wor grand to be able to see t' fire ageean. Bi t' time Ah wor eatin mi teea-cake mooast o' t'clooathes were fowlded up, an' mi two ants 'ould be darnin' stockings. Ah'd leet mi cannle an' set off upstairs, an' this time Ant Marth' Ann 'ould appen bawl after me: 'Think on! Mind tha doesn't spill onny cannle-fat on t' flooar!'

Wedn'sda (Shoppin' Day). Ivvery Wedn'sda Ant Sar' Ann went to t' Co-op an bowt all sooarts o' grooaceries — but there wer nowt tasty for dinner. It wor allus fried spuds flavoured wi a bit of o' mahse-trap cheese, what wi called wengby, cos it wor as tough as leather. T' seet on it used to mak me gip, bud Aunt Sar' Ann ewsed to stand ower me an' mak me eyt it up.

Still, there wor summat on a Wedn'sda at seeamed like a real treat — fish an' chips for teea. After Ah'd livered mi papers Ah'd ter go dahn ter t' fish-'oile. I' them days all three on us could get a meal for fowerpence-'awfpenny. Fish wor a penny, chips nobbut a 'awfpenny.

Thursda (Bakin' Day). T' best day o' t' week! Ee, Thursdas wor grand i' winter. Plenty o' coil on t' fire to get t' oven 'ot, an' when Ah come 'ooame at dinnertime, what a glooarious smell ther wor comin aht o' yond oven! Ant Sar' Ann 'ould be ewsin' t' table-top, chucking t' dooaf abaht, brayin' it wi t' rollin' pin, clahtin' it wi' 'er fist nah an' ageean, then cuttin' lumps off to fit into t' looaf tins, which she put into t' fender. While she wor waitin' for t' dooaf to rise she'd roll aht t' curn teea-cakes an set abaht makkin' fattie-cakes an' moggy. Ee, it wor grand wor all yon bakin when it come aht o' t' oven — both t' smell on it an' t' seet on it. By gum! Ivvery Thursda mi gob wattered same as its nivver done sin.

Frida (Fettlin' Day). This wor t' wust day o' t' week. Ah 'ed ter ger up an ahr sooiner an' shift all t' chairs an' t' sofa aht o' t' rooad. Bi t'time t' two ants 'ed finished, t' ahse wer rivven i' bits. Ther wor nooa fire, an t' watter 'ed ter be boiled on t' gas-ring. As sooin as Ant Marth' Ann wor off to 'er wark, Ant Sar' Ann 'ould start black-leadin' an' brasso-in', an' bi t' time Ah come ooame fer mi dinner sh'd fettled t' brass fender (t' one at they browt aht at week-ends, tha knaws) cleaned all t' orn-iments, weshed t' pot dogs on t' mantlepiece, an' polished t' knob on t' oven dooar till it shone as breet as a full mooin. Dinner wor allus t' same on Fettlin' Day — cowd meyt pie an' Yorksher Relish.

When Ah come ooame after mi paper rahnd, Aunt Marth' Ann 'ould ave just nicely finished sweepin' t' yard wi' t' besom, swillin' t' flegs an' scahrin' t' dooarst'n. Ah can 'ear 'er nah bawlin at me: 'Tha mun wipe thi feet afooare tha comes in 'ere! Dooan't thee trail onny muck into t' ahse or tha'll feel t' back o' my 'and!' Mind you, when Ah did get inside Ah will admit it allus looked reight cooasy. Ivverythin' wor streight, an' t' fire wor blazing away all breet an' friendly in t' gleamin surrahnd. Aye, even as a lad, Ah wor glad ter see t' ahse fettled.

Setterda (Laikin' Day) No schooil on a Setterda, so Ah could lig i' bed a bit longer, an mooast o' t' day Ah could do owt Ah wanted — 'appen laik at taws, or fooitball, or just mullock

As leet-gi'en as a posser-'ead.

abaht. We' 'ed sausages fer dinner of a Setterda — two apiece — wi mashed pertaties, an' as sooin as it wor ower, an t' pots wor weshed, aht 'ould come t' brass fender an' t' owd iron fender wor sided till Sunda neet. Then they'd put a plush green cover ovver t' table, wi t' aspidestra plonked i' t' middle

Sunda (Chapil Day). Sunda mornin they saw to it at Ah ed a reight gooid wesh afooare Ah put mi Sunda clooathes on. T' owd ants ewsed ter don theresens up i' ther Sunda best, wi black skirts nearly touchin' t' flooar, an' laced-up booits underneath — but yer nivver saw owt o' t' booits till they sat thersens dahn. When we set off, they'd don ther Sunda 'ats, all covered i' flahrs, an wi gurt big 'at-pins stickin' aht an lookin as if they went reight through ther 'eeads an' come aht at t' other side.

Well, they'd go ter t' chapil while Ah went ter t' Sunda schooil, an then Ah'd come 'ooame in 'igh spirits ready fer t' Sunda dinner. It wor a champion meal, even though it wor allus t' same — rooast beef an' Yorkshire puddin'. After dinner Ah could read mi comic, an t' ants 'ould read t' *Sunda Cumpanion*. Ah remember there wor nooa sahnd save t' tickin' o' t' owd grandfatther clock an' t' rustlin' o' t' paper. They'd read 'awf on it apiece, tha sees, then swap ower.

Ah'd ter gooa ter t' Sunda schooil ageean i' t' afternooin, an' they med me go wi' 'em ter t' chapil at neet. Ah dursn't mak onny complaints, bud if ivver Ah looked a bit dahn i' t' mahth abaht it, Ant Sar'Ann 'ould say: 'Tha's nooan laikin' aht on a Sunda, bud if tha be'aves thissen tha'll 'appen get some peew spice.'

Well, at awf past eight Ah ed mi biscuit an' a sup o' milk, an' as Ah med mi way up t' stairs bi t' flickerin' leet o' mi cannle, t' maiden ants 'ould start ter side t' green table-cover, swap t' brass fender fer t' iron 'n, an' put t' aspidestra back in t' winder bottom. Last of all they'd wind t' gran'fatther clock up so's it could start another wick's wark, tellin ivvery ahr o t' day, tickin' an' strikin' away ter regerlate wer clock-wark lives — t' same owd thing, wick in, an' wick aht.

Horace Kellett (WR)

This is the first story in a collection of the same name (first published in 1912) by the Rev Walter F Turner, for many years vicar of Fridaythorpe, an acute observer of local speech and ways. His quaint spelling of East Riding dialect has been retained, as has his attempt to convey the precise sounds. However, only public readings — complete with facial expressions and actions, as given by the late Jack Danby — can do it justice.

Goodies

It fair caps me what for fooaks want te it goodies i' Choch! Yan wad reallye think 'at soomm fooaks couldn't saah ther prayers wivoot a goody i' ther moothes. It caps owt! It dis, Ah seer.

T' parson o' Soondah 'ad nobbut joost getten inti t' pew, an' a fat oard woman i' t' seeat i' froont o' me thowt sher were fooast te ev a goody. An' sher parzels 'er and awaah roond tiv' er greeat oard pockit at t' back, an' began scrattin aboot, an' rattlin kays an' paaper an' sike like, te see if sher could finnd a bit o' goody. An' there sher war laatin an' scrattin aboot, like a 'en on a moock middin, wharl wer gat te t' Psalms.

An' sher gat that vexed, becos sher couldn't finnd yan o' onny sooart, sher could scaarce bard. Sher bleeamed t' bairns, yer knaw, for gerrin tiv 'er pockit throoff t' week. Sher knawed sher'd left twe or tree o't' lasst Soondah, d'yer see? or else sher wad a gettin soomm mare when sher were i' Pickering Set'dah neet; bud noo sher couldn't finnd yan, naather a mint, ner a rooase, ner a acid, ner a anise, ner owt.

Awivver sher were despert jealous sher owt te ev a goody iv er pockit soomwheres, d'yer see? Seea i' t' fosst lesson sher'd ev anoother laat. An' sher began to tak t' things oot of er pockit this tahme, d'yer see? an' put 'em doon i' t' pew ageean 'er.

By Lad! Ah wadn't like to be a woman an' nobbut a yar pockit, an' that awaah roond at t' back, where ye' etti crick yer neck an' put yer shooder oot te ger at it. Ah wadn't awivver!

Ah tell yer what, lads, if you ad seen what a greeat vasst o' things that there woman ad i' yar pockit; an' t' tewin, an' t' scrattin, an' t' twistin sher ad te ger a bit o' goody oot at warn't there, yer'd sympathahse wiv em, Ah tell yer, when ther want te ger inti, what ther call, rational costume.

Look yer! Ah couldn't fairly tell yer what there wasn't i' that there woman pockit! Ah joost shoott me ees, an' oppened 'em ageean, an' Ah thowt Ah were at a joomle saale i'steead o' i' t' Choch, Ah did awivver! Ah ev thotteen pockits me sen, an, look yer, Ah ayant as monny things i' all on 'em tegither as what that there woman ad i' urr yan, Ah seer Ah ayant.

There was t' doer kay, there was a an' ketcher, there was a bootten ook, there was a kettle odder, there was fower or fahve bits o' band, there was a thimmle, there was a pincushin, there was a posse, there was a yed measure, there was aaf a doozzen airpins lapped oopp iv a bit o' paaper — Ah knaw ther were airpins, becos sher oppened 'em oot, sher thowt t' goody ad mebbe getten amang em, d'yer see? an' there was soommat else, Ah've forgotten what. Ohr eye, there was a bit o' pencil wi' t' point brokken, an' there was a cleease pin, an' a bit o' wax, an' despert thrang deed o' boottons, an' bits o' paaper at ad mebbe ad goodies in 'em at soomm tahme, an' a deal mare things.

An' ther were all i' yar pockit! That's what capped me. Oo-an-ivver sher gat 'em in Ah deean't knaw. An' Ah were matched te knaw oo sher were gahin te ger 'em in ageean afoor t' Choch lowsed, bud awivver sher did.

An' sher went reet awaah doon inti t' boddom o' that there pock-it, an' sher rowed aboot, an' laated i' t' coorners, an' sher couldn't finnd a bit o' goody deeah what sher wad, there warn't yan.

By Lad! she did luke vexed!

An' sher began te sooart o' sooart t' things ower, an' trust 'em back intiv er pockit ageean. An' sher put t' doer kay in at t' boddom, yer knaw, becos it ud be t' fosst thing sher'd want oot — ther a straange contrairy thing is a woman — an' then sher put er anketcher in, an' then t' rist o' t' things. Awivver sher gat 'em all rammled in a deal sharper an' Ah could o' reckoned.

An' then sher leeaned back i' t' seeat te ev a rist, an' Ah's think sher wanted yan, sher were varry near tewed te deeath. An' Ah thowt sher'd deean wiv er oard pockit for yar sarvice awivver.

Bud joost as t' parson began is sarmon an' 'ad gin oot t' text, t' woman wanted 'er 'anketcher, an' sher ad te gan tiv er pockit ageean. An' sher gat odden t' anketcher be t' coorner an' raave it oot. An' t' thimmle com oot wiv it, d'yer see? An' t' thimmle rattled doon onti t' seeat, d'yer see? An, by Lad! there was a goody toommled oot o' t' thimmle!

Ah nivver seed neeabody se pleased i' me wick! Sher were fair capped, was t' woman. An' sher popped t' goody intiv er mooth, an' by Goom! it were a mint! an' a despert strang un an' all, it fair reeked all ower t' Choch! An' there sher set knappin an' knappin awaah like a steeanchecker. An' then sher stack a bit on't awaa inti t' coorner of er cheek, te mak it lasst, an' listened te t' sarmon mebbe a minute, or mebbe twea. An' then sher started scroonchin awaa ageean, like an' oard ratten at t' back of a skettin booard, wharl sher'd getten it deean.

An' then sher tooke t' thimmle oot ageean, te see if there were onny mare goodies getten in, but there warn't.

An' afoor Ah knawed where Ah war, t' sarmon was owerd wiv, an' all Ah'd eeard on't was t' text, 'Tak neeah thowt for the morrer'. An' seeah wer coommed awaa oot. An' Ah knaw t' oard woman were thinkin all t' tahme sher'd etti ev soomm mare goodies getten afoor t' next Soondah.

Oh, them goodies! Ah deean't knaw what maks fooaks se craazed on 'em, Ah deean't, Ah seer. Noo Ah can chow mah bit o' bacca i' t' Choch an' nivver mak a soond wiv it, an' nivver neeabody knaw nowt at all aboot it.

Walter F Turner (ER)

From The Colne Valley Almanack (1932), this is a little satire on a performance of Handel's Messiah, *unfailingly performed every year in many West Riding chapels and churches, and in particular by the celebrated Huddersfield Choral Society. Read in authentic style by Arthur Kinder of Honley, this was a popular reading at YDS meetings.*

Goin' to t' Messiah

Two Golcar chaps were walking down Scar Lane one cold December day, when one said:

'Ah'm thinkin' o' goin' to t' *Messiah* i' th' Huddersfild Taan Hall next Friday neet. Will ta go wi mi, Bill?'

Brass or silver bands — a typical Yorkshire sound.

'Nay, music's nowt i' my line. Ah like a gooid comic song or a lively jig, but Ah mek nowt o' this sacred stuff, as they call it. It's a bit aboon me. An' Ah reckon there'll be nooan o' yar sooart there; mostly religious folk and swells donned i' boiled shirts, an' women wi' nowt mich on. Now, tha mun goa bi thiseln, and tell me all abaat it some time.'

During the following week these pals met again, when the following conversation took place:

'Oh, it wor champion, lad. Ah wodn't ha missed it for a dollar. When Ah gate theear t' Taan Hall were craaded, choc full o' folk; t' organ chap were laakin' abaat like wi t' organ, playing nowt perticlar, nobbut running his fingers up an' daan as if he wor practisin', like yar Martha used to do when shoo started learnin' ta play t' piano. Then they brought t' Messiah in — at ony rate what Ah took ta be it. It wor t' biggest instrument on t' platform, an' it wor covered wi' a green bag. When they'd takken it aat o' t' bag, a chap rubbed it belly wi' a stick, an' tha sud ha' yerd it groaan. It wor summat like t' last expirin' mooan of a dying caa. It worn't mich better when he started t' twitchin' it yeroil up, an' in a bit a chap came on donned in a white waistcoit an' everything wor as quiet as a maase.

'He 'ad a stick, an' he used it an' all to some tune, Ah'll tell thi. If tha asks me, he ought ta ha' walloped some o' them chaps 'at wor reckonin' ta sing. They hadn't been goin' long afore they wor fratchin' like cats. One side said they wor t' King o' glory, and' t' other side said *they* wor, so which side really won Ah've no idea. Ah think they ought to ha' gooan to Leeds Road next day and settled it theer.

'Then there wor a bit o' bother abaat some sheep 'at wor lost. Ah don't know who they belonged to, but they must ha' been champion twisters and turners judgin' bi t' words an' fancy music. One lot o' singers must ha been very fond o' mutton, because they kept on saying "All we like sheep". Ah couldn't help saying to a chap sat next to me "It's all reight is sheep i' moderation, but gi me a bit o' beef underdone". He looked daggers at me and said "Shush!". So Ah shushed.

'In a bit a big chap gat on his feet an' started singin. Ah wish tha could ha heeard him. He'd a voice like owd Jabez

Shaw, o' Linfit, who once freetened all t' folk on Blackpool Promenade when he went to t' top o' t' Tower an' started shaatin' "View, Alloa!", just like he did when he wor huntin on Blackmoorfooit. Well, this chap wor as mad as blazes, an' singin summat abaat t' heathen ragin together, an' t' band wor just as furious, they saiged away at ther fiddles whol Ah'm certain ther arms warked.

'Ah wor feelin a bit stiff an' a bit stalled Ah'm baan to confess, when everybody i' t' audience stood up, an' t' band an' singers an' a chap wi a long trumpet, started t' Halleluyah Chorus. By gum, lad, it wor fair grand. It med mi back go into cold shivers, specially when they said it wor baan to rain for ivver an' ivver. Ah'd had mi bob's worth, so Ah pushed mi way aat, an' made mi way to t' station afore t' rain came on, as Ah'd forgotten mi umbrella.'

A short and sometimes funnier version of the above was written by Arthur Jarratt, published in the 1985 YDS Summer Bulletin.

A farmer was given a ticket to a performance of *Messiah*. He had not heard it, or any other oratorio before, and this is how he described it to a neighbour:

'Well noo t' spot was ommost full, an' Ah'd a job ti finnd missen a seeat. Hooiver, Ah did, an' then they started ti fill up t' platform wiv a lot o chaps all dressed up i' white shot fronts. They leeaked as thaw they'd all left their weskits at yam. Hooiver they'd aall gotten a fiddle apeeace, an' mah wod, they did leeak grand!

Noo when they were all sattled doon, they browt in a sooalin greeat creeatur iv a greean bag. They took aall his clooas off, then they screwed up his lugholes wahl he fairly creeaked. Then they scraaped a white stick ower his chest, an' by lad, thoo nivver heeard siken a grooan.

Then a lartle chap cummed in wiv a stick iv his hand, and started ti waave it aall ower spot, and some moore chaps i' white dickies thowt he'd gone balmy way they leeaked at him. Sooa they shooted at him aboot some sheeap that ed gotten lost. Ah deeant knaw hoo monny on 'em there was, or what they were woth, but yan thing was sartin — they'd aall gotten lost.

Then a chap got up an' sung by hissen. Ah think they must a bin his sheeap somebody ed tekken, cos he said they imagined a vaan thing. He soonded raavin mad — an' t' organist he soonded mad an' aall. Ah wor glad when fella sat hissen doon.

Then a lot of women got owerend. They aall lewked as though they wor gettin on a bit. They sang "Unto Us A Child is Born" and t' fellas at t' other end shooted back "Wonderful! Wonderful!" An' Ah thowt t' saame. There wasn't yan on 'em under sixty.

Then a chap stood up an' said he was t' King o' Kings, and then another said *he* was — an' they started faallin oot. Then

The clog, once the standard footwear for young and old.

'E couldn't stop a pig in a ginnel.

when t' audience all stood up ti see what was t' matther they sang "Halleluyah! It's off ti raain for ivver and ivver!"

Ah thowt bi this Ah'd had plenty, so Ah got mi hat and med for dooer. Ah thowt Ah'd better get yam afoor t' flood caame. It was a good do tho. But Ah do hoaap them sheeap tonned up.'

Arthur Jarratt (ER)

One of the most popular long-running dialect series was the one written under the pen-name of 'Buxom Betty' by Emily Denby, born and bred at Tong Park, Baildon. She started it soon after joining the staff of the Bradford Telegraph and Argus *in 1919, turning out weekly stories for almost thirty years. Her dialect was keenly observed and faithfully rendered, delighting readers who saw their very own vernacular and everyday life in print. Here are some samples from the vast output of 'Buxom Betty'.*

Some Gooid Luck fer T' Higginbottoms

T' Higginbottam fam'ly wor just beginnin' o' ther teea t' other evenin', all but Willyam Henery, an' he wor t' last to come in, as ewsal.

When he did land, he left t' door wide oppen, an' slumped intuv his place by t' twins, an' reiched ovver ter a slice o' butter an' cake.

His mother landed him a slap i' t' lug, an' Willyam Henery pooled a face.

'Goa wesh them hands afore tha touches owt t' eyt,' shoo commanded. 'Tha mud ha' been up t'chimley ivver sin t' schooil lowsed. An' put wood in t' 'oile! Haw monny times hev Ah telled tha abaht thi manners? Tha mud ha' been browt up on t' top o' Rumalds Moor, tha's that rough an' iggerant. Frame thissen, an' doan't let me ha' to tell tha ageean, er tha goas to bed baht teea, soa tha knaws.'

Willyam Henery sidled to t' door, an' clashed it tul, an' then went into t' scullery to wesh his hands. As he wiped t' muck off on to t' towel, he saw summat slip rahnd t' pantry door, an' he sang aht.

'Mother, ther's a black cat i' t' pantry. It must be a lost un. Mun Ah pawse it aht?'

'It'll hev comed in when tha left t'door oppen.' said his mother. 'Mak it goa, I want na thievin' cats i' my pantry.'

'Nay, mother,' said Doris Mary, 'a black cat's lucky, they say; yo moan turn it aht,' an' shoo jumped up an' ran to lewk at it.

'Puss, puss, come here then,' shoo said; 'ticin' it into t' kitchen. 'Ee, lewk mother; isn't it a bonny un? Ah I wonder what made it come tuv ahr house?'

'It'll hev smelled mi fatther kipper, said Jane Ellen. 'Gie it a bit, fatther, an' then you'll join t' luck it ha' browt.'

Missis Higginbottam gav it some milk in a saucer, an' it supped it, ah' sat itsen dahn o' t' hearthrug i' t' front o' 'fire, an' began o' weshin' it whiskers 'n' made itsen at hoam. Joaseph and Joasephine stroaked it 'n' made a fuss on't, an' t' cat seemed to like it.

'Let's keep it, mother,' said Jane Ellen. "Ah knaw we s'll be lucky wi' it.'

'We can dew wi' all t' gooid luck it can bring us,' said Missis Higginbottam, 'but Ah'm no a believer i' sich like owd wife tales. Hahiver, if t' thing behaves itsen, it can stop toneet, an' happen it'll finnd it way hoam i' t' mornin' to wheer it belongs.'

Soa t'cat stopped wheer it wor, but at t' last thing Missis Higgibottam oppened t' house door, an' t' cat walked aht, an' shoo locked up an' hoaped shoo'd seen t' last on't.

Hahiver, shoo hedn't, fer t' thing walked in t' next mornin' an' axed fer some breakfast as if it hed a reight. It went in an' aht freely all t' day, an' t' lasses an' t' twins wor as suited as owt cos ther 'luck' wor stoppin' wi' 'em.

That neet, t' twins laiked wi' t' cat on t' rug, an' it seemed to like ther comp'ny well. Joasephine tried to don it a dolly frock on, an' then it clawked her an' ran under t' dresser aht o' t' gate.

'Tha sud ha' letten t' thing aloan,' said her mother as shoo lapped t' wounded hand up. 'It'll noan mell on tha if tha keeps off on't.'

All wor peeace an' quietness fer happen hawf an hahr, an' Obadiah wor noddin' in his chair when his missis, whoa'd heen intuv her neighbour's — Missis Nimbletongue's — landed in an' says. 'Nay, deng it Obadiah, Ah'll be felled if tha tha wodn't sit t' fire aht if Ah worn't here to mend it. Pop dahn into t' cellar an' fotch us a skep o' coil up, Ah mun ha' some fer mornin', Ah've a pie to bake.'

Obadiah grummled under his breeath, gat up an' went dahn t' cellar.

'Tak a leet,' said his missis, but Obadiah tewk no gaum on her, an' went baht.

He filled t' coil skep, an' wor just settin' off up t' steps wi' it when he trayd o' summat soft. 'Ther wor a squawk an' a yowl, an' summat grabbed his enkle an' seemed to ram hawf-a-dozen red-hot darnin' needles in, an' it wor his turn to yowl. He threw t' bucket o' coils dahn an' swore, as t' black cat shot past him up t' steps. He'd ha' landed it into t' street theer an' then, but he couldn't finnd it, cos it hed getten aht o' t' gate to nurse it damaged tail.

'Gooid luck!' he grummled. 'Ah'll give it gooid luck if Ah catch it.'

T' cat wor theer t' next mornin', an' it hed sattled dahn as if it hed nivver hed knawn another hoam.

That afternooin Miss Higginbottam wor reight threng dewin' her chaymers. It was a grand day, an' shoo'd riven all t' carpets up an' hed 'em aht o' doors an' gie'en 'em a gooid airin', an' shoo fotched 'em in an' tewk 'em back an' gat 'em all dahn an' straightened. Shoo set off dahn t' chaymer steps, an' hed getten hawfway when t' cat gat under her feet. There wor a minglin' o' shrikes as boath Missis Higginbottam an' t' cat landed to t' boddom in a heeap.

'Haw dearie me!' shoo moaned as shoo sammed hersen up. 'Ah thowt Ah wor killed. Deng thee, if tha comes owt near ma ageean today, Ah'll pawse mi fooit throo tha.'

T' cat didn't come near her, an' noab'dy saw it that evenin', ner t' next mornin' nawther, an' they all decided 'at it hed goan away to wheer it hed comed throa. It wor Jane Ellen 'at discovered it when shoo went upstairs to get ready fer a donce shoo wor goin' tul.

'Mother,' shoo sang aht in a agitated voice. 'Mother, just come an' lewk. That theer blessed cat hez three kittens i' t' box

Put t' wood in t' 'oile!

wheer Ah keep mi blue silk frock. It's made a bed on 't.'

It hed, an' ther wor nowt for it but to mak t' best o' things woll t' kitlins could crawl abaht. Then boath t'cat an' them hed to goa; t' greengroacer man tewk 'em, cos he wor plagued wi' mice.

'Black cats is lucky, yo' knaw missis,' he said, but Missis Higginbottam said he wor welcome ter all t' luck they browt him.

'We've hed ahr share, lad!' shoo said.

Emily Denby (WR)

T' Naybors Maks Merry

'Ah's it lewkin' this mornin', think yo?' inquired Missis Higginbottam ov her naybor, Missis Nimbletongue, as shoo hung t' mop aht to dry on a nail bi t' kitchen door, just as Missis Nimbletongue com aht ov her house to shak a duster.

'Haw, it's i' reight fettle, Ah lewked at it last neet,' said Missis Nimbletongue 'Ah sud ommost think it's ready fer bottlin' nah. Come yor ways in, an' see.'

Missis Higginbottam slipped aht of her awn back gate an' in at her naybor's, an' they boath went solemnly dahn into t' Nimbletongue's cellar, wheer Missis Nimbletongue lifted a claht off of a gurt bakin' bowl an' revealed a dark, seethin' pool o' strange liquor 'at hed a still stronger smell.

'Aye, it's ready,' agreed Missis Higginbottam. 'All hoap it'll be all reight. We've kept it nice an' quiet an' ther's noab'dy knaws abaht it nobbut wersens. It'll be a reight capper when we bring it aht at Kersmas. It'll lick all ther bottles o' cheap port wine.'

'It will that,' said Missis Nimbletongue. 'Mi owd mother ewsed to allus mak her awn wine, an' real stingo it wor an' all. Two glasses wod knock a strong man ovver, an' even mi fatther ewsed to stegger a bit when he'd hed a drop. Ah nobbut hoap this'll be as gooid.'

'Well, Ah'll get mi bottles ready,' said Missis Higginbottam, an' this afternoooin when all's quiet an' t' inner threng owered we'll get t' job done an' t' bottles sided aht o' t' gate.'

'Nah then,' said Missis Nimbletongue, 'Ah s'll be ready when ye are,' an' oft went Missis Higginbottam to finish her jobs an' get t' dinner goin'.

As sooin as ivver t' threng wor owered an' t' dinner pots weshed up an' sided, Missis Higginbottam sammed abaht a score o' empty bottles together aht o' t' cellar an' clapped 'em intuv a basket, an' off sho sailed into t' next door.

Missis Nimbletongue tewk a cup an' a jug aht o' t' cupboard an' dahn they went into t' cellar to tun ther wine.

'It'll be cleearer underneyth when we've skemmed t' top off,' said Missis Nimbletongue, an' shoo proaceeded to dew this, an' then shoo decided 'at they sud lift t' bowl up an' hug it up into t' kitchen. They tewk hod on't, an' managed to land it upstairs baht spillin' onny er shakkin' it up ta mich.

Fotchin' two glasses aht o' t' cupboard, Missis Nimbletongue filled 'em, an' handed one tuv her naybor an' said 'Good health,' an' they boath supped off.

'Ah-h-h!' exclaimed Missis Higginbottam, 'but that's grand stuff, it's fair wahrmin'.'

'Aye, it puts new life intuv a body,' said Missis Nimbletongue.

'Them twoathri grapes an' raisins we put in hez fair made it taste o' sunshine. Let's hev another sup.'

They did dew, an' then they gat agate an' strained an' sieved t' mixtur, an' ivvery like they kept hevin' another sup. It browt back t' memories o' owd times to Missis Nimbletongue in' shoo started o' tellin' all maks o' tales o' t' days goan by, an' shoo waxed roamantic an' talked abaht her coartin' davs an' nawther o' t' ladies noaticed hah t' time wor flyin'. It wor rayther dry wark talkin', an' they kept fillin' ther glasses up an' suppin' one anent t' other, an' Missis Higginbottam, who 'ed been a bit ov a gaston as a young lass, gat agate o' tellin' t' tale ov her goins-on, an' they boath gat reight merry 'at t' recollections they'd hed.

Missis Nimbletongue hed been a bit ov a sinner, an' shoo sang a bit ov a ditty 'at hed been a reight favrite o' Rasmus's

A pit-head, when Yorkshire coal was king.

when they wor coartin'. Shoo'd getten into t' second verse when ther wor a rattle an' a clatter at t' door.

'Is mi mother here?' called aht Willyam Henery Higginbottam.

'Ee doy, is it soa near teeatime?' gasped Missis Higginbottam. 'Ah'd noa ideea, Slip into t' house an' mend t' fire an' pop t' kettle on, wilta? An' gie t' twins a slice o' tracle an' breead apiece, an' Ah'll be in directly.'

Willyam Henery ran to dew as he wor telled, an' t' two ladies went o wi' ther task o' fillin' an' strainin', an' ivery nah an' then suppin' t' wine.

'Theer, ther's nobbut much left, nohbu t' dregs,' said Missis Nimbletongue. 'Ah think we'll leeave that drop to settle, an' we'll hev another glass apiece afore we side t' bottles away. Here's tiv us, all on us, may we nivver want nowt, noan on us, ner me nawther,' an' they boath drained ther' glasses.

Missis Higginbottam popped her scarf on to goa hoam, but shoo bethowt hersen ov another merry tale to tell afore shoo went, an' then Missis Nimbletongue hed a tale to cap it, an' they laughed an' laughed, an' just then in walked Doris Mary Higginbottam.

'Is mi mother here?' an' Jane Ellen follered her.

'Ee fer sewer!' shoo exclaimed.

'Whativer are yo' dewin', mother? Noa teea ready an' all on us waitin' mi fatther's goin' ranty.'

'Ah'm comin', lass,' said Missis Higginbottam. 'Ee, whativer time is it, Ah can't see t' clock face reight, it seems to hev hands all rahnd.'

Shoo gat up to goa, an' then sat her dahn ageean, an' just then Rasmus walked in.

'By Gow, Ah dew feel queer,' said Misssis Higginbottam, 'Fotch ahr Obadiah, some'dy,' an' Rasmus hed ter click hod ov his missis as shoo set off to pop t' kettle on. 'Ee, Ah'm bahn to hev a dizzy gurd,' sho gasped.

Doris Mary ran hoam fer her fatther, an' Jane Ellen lewked 'at her mother an' then at Missis Nimbletongue, an' then at t' jug an' t' bottles, an' sho didn't knaw whether to laugh er roar.

Obadiah landed in, an' wor a minut er two afore he tummled

to what wor up. Then him an' Rasmus lewked at one another, an' Rasmus gurned same as a mule at a thistle.

'Well, Ah'll be felled!' said Obadiah, an' his missis mooaned aht 'Tak me hoam, lad, Ah doan't feel at all weel.'

Obadiah tewk hod on her an' off they went, an' when shoo gat into t' house shoo said: 'Lowse us mi shooin off an' Ah'll goa to bed.'

T' next mornin' it wor ommost dinnertime afore t' naybors saw owt o' one another, an' when they did happen to see one another ovver t' backyard wall, Missis Nimbletongue said: 'What abaht yor share o' bottles?', an' Missis Higginbottam lewked at her an' said: 'Doan't mention t' bottles ter me today. Ah'm ower poorly. It'll tak ma woll Kersmas to lewk onny mak o' a bottle i' t' face ageean. It yo've getten 'em into t' cellar aht o' t' seet, let 'em stop theer. Hev yo' owt to cure a heeadwark?'

'Ah've ta'en a couple o' hasprins,' said Missis Nimbletongue, 'an' Ah'v turned teetoatal an' all. Ah s'll mak na more wine. Them 'at wants it can mak ther awn fer t' future.'

Emily Denby (WR)

J Fairfax-Blakeborough, son of Richard (see page 34), continued his father's expertise in dialect by writing a series of tales for the Ackrill group of papers based in Harrogate. Though the narrative is in Standard English, the conversation gives a real flavour of country life in North Yorkshire before the Second World War, as in this example.

Mary Thompson taks t' Cramp

'Is awd Mary Thompson gahin ti mak a speech?' asked Matty Pearson on seeing the lady mentioned suddenly jump up in the Ripon market bus.

'Sha leeaks despert savage aboot summat,' replied Lizzie Leckonby, and at that moment the bus pulled up with a jerk, throwing Mary against Rachel Raby who indignantly shouted 'Mind my corns! What are ya doing, ringin' t' bell? You don't want ti be oot yet!'

Mrs Thompson made no apology, but uttered a succession of big 'O's and little 'o's in an agonised tone. The conductress called out 'Come along if you're getting off!', the driver peered from his seat into the bus, and the vicar's wife explained to the conductress that Mrs Thompson, to steady herself, had had her hand on the bell without knowing it.

'Sit doon, Mrs Thompson, an' stop makkin' nasty faces, you've set Tilda's bairn off blutherin' wi' fright,' said Lizzie Leckonby.

'I don't think Mrs Thompson is very well,' remarked the vicar's wife.

'Are ya seized wi' them gallopin' pains inwardly, or what?' demanded Rachel Raby, whose basket of eggs had been, and still were, in danger.

Suddenly, Mary Thompson's face gained its usual hard composure; she sat down, and then explained to Rachel that she had been seized with cramp in her leg 'summat cruel'.

'Mun I come an' massidge it for ya, Mary,' called out Matty Pearson. 'I'se a St John's Ambliance man noo, ya knaw, an' knaws all oboot fosst aid an' sike like.'

'You can give fosst aid when you're assed fer it,' retorted Mrs Thompson indignantly, adding, 'If you had what I have, you wadn't think it a laughing or joking matter. Ah was seized i' bed last night wi' cramp i' baith my big toes. They stood straight up like guide-possts, an' Ah was sure Ah was strucken that way fer life. Ah can tell ya they gave me jip. When Ah gits cramp i' me leg, Ah'se boond ti stand up, whether it's i' chotch or in a bus.'

'Ah can't give ya neea comfort,' said Lizzie Leckonby, 'it'll end i' you bein' strucken doon a lifeless corpse … but there's neea need ti pull sike faces ez what you did just now. It's nut, in a way o' speakin', becomin' in a public place, hupsettin' ivverybody, stoppin' the bus, an' varry nigh sittin' flop doon on Rachel's eggs. Even if folks has cramp, they wants ti try an' conduck the'r selves proper and remember the'r manners.'

'Mind my eggs! Tossin' yer airms aboot like a flay-crow,' exclaimed Rachel Raby who went on, 'If you're gahin' ti hev onny mair attacks o' cramp let me knaw, an' I'll ask Robert there ti give me his seat. They tell me cramp's fetched on wi' bad seccelation, that'll be why Matty says you should run up an' doon t' bank side. It's wo'th tryin.'

Mary has also got what she calls 'varry-cooarse veins,' and the whole village knows about it. Although she is what she terms 'under the doctor,' she has asked all and sundry for a cure. Lizzy Leckonby told her quite plainly:

'Ah can't give you no comfort. A party what gits varry-cooarse veins at your time o' life — fer you must be a big age — has 'em fer keeps.'

Later, however, Lizzie 'bethowt herself', and when Matty Pearson remarked 'It's a bad job aboot Mary,' Lizzie said 'You can tell her that Ah yance heearded of someyan who cured theirsens by sitting for a hower with their legs above their heads night an' morning. Tell awd Mary ti try that, an' ti let you know when she'll start ti perform, then we'll baith gan an' peep through the winder, an' set a cracker off, or you can let oot a greeat sneeze or summat o' that there.'

When Matty delivered the first part of the message, Mary was most indignant. 'It may be all right for an indelingcate party like that next door ti sit with the'r legs above the'r heads, but Ah hasn't come ti sike ingusting conduck yit! Ah nivver heeared sike an undecent suggeshun. Where should Ah be if the vicar walked in an' fan me i' sike a position?'

'You'd be iv yer chair wi' yer legs up ovver yer head, and I'll gallantee t' vicar wadn't stop ter look twice — he'd be off like a scalded cat.'

J Fairfax-Blakeborough (NR)

YORKSHIRE DIALECT CLASSICS

A remarkable dialect monologue written by Gwen Wade (1904-96), born in Ilkley, later running a dairy farm at Ripon and becoming a vice-president of the YDS, for whom she edited an anthology of West Riding verse.

Death and Annie Maria

Eh Nu'ss, it's tha! Eh Nu'ss, Ah's pleased tha's coom — Ah feel reight aht o' missen, Ah dew that. It's mi rigg at maks me wankly-lahk, it warks that bad! Ah'd getten t gangerine i' mi fooit, tha knaws, an' they tewk mi leg off ... bud they cann't tak me rigg off, can they, Nu'ss! ...

Next mornin' t' 'eead doctor-chap cooms rahnd t' wards wi' t' Sister. By! Bi' t' carry-on they mad fer 'im, 'e might ha' bin t' Lord Almighty Hissen.

'Nah then, Mrs Binks', 'e says, 'An' how are we?'

'Ah's reight eniff', Ah says, 'an' smilin' yet. Did yer reckon ter finnd me roarin' lahk a barn?' Ah ses tiv 'im. If ye did, ye're mistakken — Ah'm noan that sooart!'

Laff! They fair brasst wi' laffin' at me ... bud Ah kept theer spirits up in theer, Ah did that!

'How old are you, Mrs Binks?', he says.

'Eighty-three coom September, young man', Ah tellt him, 'An' Ah've seen more mucky days in mi tahm than all t' lot of yer standin' on yer 'eeads, an' Ah'm laffin' yet.'

Eh Nuss, Ah dew feel badly ... Hod mi hand ageean whol this lot's ower, willta? ... Ah get reight muzzy efter these 'ere dews, Nuss; th'll nivver credit it, bud a bit back Ah thowt Ah seed Ahr lahtle lad i' t' door-oile theer — 'im at we lost wi' t' fever. It wor nobbut a bo'd on t' doorstun, an' it fliew up an' left t' dark shadder of its wings on t' wall, lahk it mowt ha' bin t' Angil o' Deeath fotchin' me ...

Ah reckon Ah'll noan last ser lang, Nu'ss; Ah can feel missen slippin', lahk ...

Hod mi 'eead a bit, Nuss, it's warkin' ageean ... Nay, Ah willent ligg mi dahn! Ee! Ah can sit up ter welcome t' squire, Ah'll sit up fer t' Lord an' all! ... Ah wunner, couldsta thoil ter lewk ter mi owd cat, Nuss, tha er thi sister? Missis Brahn reckons shoo can't abide its yowlin', bud it onnly yowls cos t' vary sahnd an' smell o' Missis Brahn puts it past itself. Ah'd ha lahked owd Moses ter've ganned at front o' me, bud t' Lord God is merciful, even wi' Tom cats, so Ah mun see an' trust Him ...

Eh, an' theer's Martha, Nuss! Her an' me's bin thicker ner twins this sixty year, an' Ah'm fleered ter leave 'er with hersen. Ah can call ter mind once over she wor i' terrible trouble, an' t' thowt o' tellin' her mother wor nigh killin' 'er. Ah wor weshin at Monda mornin' when Ah 'eeard 'er shahtin' o' me: 'Annie Maria! Annie Maria!' An' Ah ses: 'Hod on, Ah'm coomin', Lass!' An' wi' that Ah drops t' peggy an' sets off laupin' fer t' river more 'n' a mile off. Did ivver yer hear t' lahks o' yon! An' when Ah wor getten theer, all flummoxed an' aht o' puff, Ah seed summat liggin' on t' benk, an' mi heart tu'ned ower i' mi breast. It wor Martha sowsed wi river watter, an' coomin aht ev a swound. Shoo lewks at me, despert-lahk, an' shoo ses: 'Annie Maria, Annie Maria! Whyfor cudn't tha let me be? Ah'd ha' doon it bud fer thee! Ah'd coom nigh on ter t' deepest bit when tha said: "Od on, Ah'm coomin', Lass!" an' lugged me backards bi' t' skutt' ...

Ah tewk 'er 'oam an' 'er mother wor reight grand wi' 'er, an' Ah've said nowt tiv 'er ner onnibody, then ner since ... us's bin thicker ner twins this sixty year ... Nay! If it in't ma lad ageean, keekin' in thruff t' door-oil! Coom thi weays in, tha lathtle good-fer nowt . .. an' ... let me ... wesh .. thi ... fea —

Gwen Wade (WR)

From the years of the second World War this is a fine comic piece of prose by Ian Dewhirst (see page 79), absolutely realistic in style and idiom, the work of a Keighley man speaking his native tongue.

Hitler is a Bad Un

Durin' t' Wahr Ah kept this big blue budgie. Joey, Ah called him. T' time Ah fun aht he could speyk wor one day when t' gas-man called, an' says 'Good mornin', Missus', but Ah didn't answer him for Ah'd summat burnin' i' t' oven an' Aw wor just lewkin' to see what it wor. When t' gas-man wor goin', he ses, 'When Ah cum in, Missus, tha didn't say owt, did ta? Well, summat did. Summat said good mornin'.'

Ah says, 'Aw've a budgie, but Ah didn't knaw he spak.' So Ah seys, 'Good mornin', Joey', an' he says, 'Good morning! Good morning!' like a proper little gentleman — lovely big blue budgie, he wor. 'Good morning! Good morning!'

Well, after that he gat to say all soarts. He used to say, 'What're yer doin' nah, Enid?' — this wor a little lass Ah used to minnd of a mornin' while her mother wer warkin'. Shoo wor nobbut three, an' Ah used to gie her mi button-box to laik wi', an' when Ah codn't hear t' buttons rattlin' Ah used to say, 'What're yer doin' nah, Enid?' Soa then, Joey used to say, 'What're yer doin' nah, Enid?' as plain as owt. He used to say, 'Pretty Jean has goan to schooil' an' all — that wor mi little niece — 'Pretty Jean has goan to schooil.'

Aw hed to hev a gert big green blinnd at t' winder i' them days, for t' black-aht, an ivvery mornin' Aw hed it to winnd up. Allus, when Ah wor winndin' it, Ah used to say, 'Hitler is a bad un!' Aye, ivvery mornin', 'Hitler is a bad un!' as Ah wor winndin' t' blinnd up. An' it worn't lang afore Joey wor sayin', 'Hitler is a —' an' then he'd stop. Just 'Hitler is a —. Hitler is a —.'

For wiks Ah tried to get him to say 'bad un', but he wodn't, though he'd say 'Hitler is a —. Hitler is a —' monny a time a day. Ah thowt happen he codn't say t' letter 'b', but he said 'Little Boy Blue' plain eniff (though Ah nivver gat him to say 'Come blow up yer horn'). He sahnded t' letter 'b's wonderful i' 'Little Boy Blue'.

Soa Ah gat to think he wor a reight Hitler man, wor Joey. He wodn't call him a bad un, at nowt. Just 'Hitler is a — . Hitler is a — .'

Well, one mornin' Ah were feelin' reight aht o' sooarts, an' when Ah wor winndin' t' blinnd up, Ah doan't knaw hah it wor, but it just slipped aht, an' Ah just says, 'Hitler is a bugger!' Ah nobbut said it once, tha knaws, it just slipped aht cos Ah wor feelin' aht o' sooarts, an' o' course Ah wor in o' mi awn.

But t' next thing Ah knew, Joey wor sayin' 'Hitler is a bugger! Hitler is a bugger!' as clear as a bell. Ah codn't shut him up at nowt, an' he wor allus sayin' it, reight through to t'end o' t' Wahr! Aye … Hitler is a bugger!'

Ian Dewhirst (WR)

There are many dialect tales about doctors (eg 'Nay,' he says, 'It's nooan brokken — it's nobbut a fracksher'*) and remedies, especially home cures, as remembered here by Muriel Shackleton.*

Gooise Greease an' Brahn Paper

When it gets rahnd ta t' back-end, winter dunt seem so far off, does it, an' t' other day Ah fun missen thinkin abaht t' owld-feshioned winters when Ah wor a nipper. ('Appen it wer walkin ower t' owld spots at set me on.)

I' them days we didn't ev jabs for flu an' 'oopin' cough, but wer mothers did t' best they could ta keep off t' coughs an' cowlds, an' owt else 'at wer goin'. They couldn't afford to ave us poorly any mooar than they could 'elp. The'd t' doctor bills ta pay then, tha knows, an' t' medicine ta pay for an' all.

If Ah'd been smittled, 'at t' first sign of a peff, or a sniffie, aht came t' camphor begs. An' it didn't matter ah much we begged an' pleaded, t' denged things were pinned on ta wer vests. Just in case ther's a few young uns 'at knows nowt abaht camphor begs, Ah'll explain. T' camphor wor i' blocks, abaht an inch square, an' 'appen abaht a quarter of an inch thick. Mi mother med little begs aht o' bits of owld wool vests, or jerseys, or summat o' t' sooart, an' popped a piece o' camphor in each one. Then t' begs wi t' camphor inside were pinned ta wer vests — wi' a safety pin.

If onnybody bumped ya on your chest, sometimes t' pin came undone, and then ya 'ad a prick ta add ta your misery, cos as sooin as t' other kids cottoned on 'at ya were wearin' camphor, they didn't 'alf torment ya. Tha sees, as sooin as t' camphor wahrmed up, it began ta smell — that wer t' idea, like — t' fumes were supposed ta clear your tubes an' keep t' germs at bay.

Nah, if ya did get a bad chest, ya were rubbed wi' camphorated oil, aht of a blue bottle, wi' ridges dahn it. Then ya ad a flannil pinned ta t' inside a your vest, ta keep it clean, an' ta keep your chest wahrm at same time. But t' flannil didn't ·keep t' stink in. T' other kids soon knew who ad camphorated oil on ther chest, an' didn't the' let ya know abaht it!

But t' worst o' t' lot were gooise greease an' brahn paper. By! That wor a torment. When t'paper got a bit rumpled it pricked, an' as sooin as onnybody heard it crackle, they thumped ya on your chest, just to 'ear it agen. They didn't ahf pester ya in t' playgrahnd when ya 'ad ta 'ave brahn paper on your chest. Ah think sometimes we 'ad a flannil on, an' all. It wor like walkin abaht i' a suit of armour.

Just for a while there wor a feshion i wearing Iodine Lockits. Does anybody else remember 'em? Ah think they were advertised in t' paper an' fowk sent up for 'em. They didn't stink like camphor, an' some o t' kids swanked a bit like, an' pulled 'em aht ta show 'em off. They were rahnd, 'appen as big as an owld penny, or was it a ha'pny? Onnyroad, they were rahnd an' were hung rahnd yer neck on a bit o' band.

Sometimes when we 'ad a cough, mi muther 'd put a spooinful o' blackcurrant jam in t' bottom of a mug, an' pour 'ot watter on it. Nah that med a varry nice drink. We'd tek as much o' that as we got chance on.

An' then they used ta give us 'olibut liver oil, an' Scott's Emulsion — ta keep up wer strength in t' winter time, an' if we did get run dahn, the' wor Parrish's Liquid Chemical Food. That turned your teeath black if ya didn't cleean 'em straight away. Ah think it were t' iron in it.

Wor it durin' t'Wahr 'at we were towld 'at turnip jewse wor good for cowlds an' sore throats? We 'ad that an' all. Ya cut t' top off a turnip an' scooped aht some o' t' middle, an' then put some brahn sugar in, an'put t' top back on agen, like a lid. T' sugar drew t' jewse aht, an' it wont bad tastin' nawther. O' course, that 'at 'ad been scooped aht o' t' middle wont thrown away — it went inta t' next dinner. Fowk 'ad ta watch points i' them days, when there were no National Health and no Fam'ly Allahance or owt like that.

Muriel Shackleton (WR)

The writer of the long-running series of 'Seth and Tom' stories on Radio York, Michael Park (see page 89) here gives an account of his childhood experience of Mischief Night (4th November), a strong tradition in the West Riding and other parts, such as in this North Yorkshire village.

Mischief Neet

Ah knaws the' still hev Mischief Neet theease days, bud it's got a bad neeame wi all t' wanton damage 'at's done. When Ah were a lad, it were just mischief, an' owd fooak were left alone. It were t' yan neet in oor village when things cam alive. It used ti start aroond awf past six, when t' young uns 'd swipe all t' yats from t' hooses an' dump 'em on someone's front lawn. Then t' owder lads 'd gan oot an get up ti all sooarts.

Ah mind yan tahm when we tried ti nick a farm yat. It were reet heavy an' it took fower on us ti lift it. We'd just got it off t' hinges when t' dooar oppens an' a dog cums runnin' oot. We dropped yon yat an' ran. Ah went off lahk a bat oot of 'ell, wi t' dog yappin' at mi heels. Them luminous socks were all t' rage at that tahm, an' Ah reckon ma yeller uns must hev shone oot lahk traffic leets! Ah took ti t' fields, an' it weren't till Ah'd lost awf mi cooat linin' on a barbed-wire fence at Ah managed ti shek t' dog off.

Black treacle were anither trick. T' idee was ti daub t' stuff on dooarknobs, knock an' run. Me an' mi mate did a whole street yance, an' after a quick dash doon t' road, ringin' an' knockin', we went ti his hoose ti avoid gettin caught. Daft beggar mun hev hed a brainstorm or summat, cos he'd put t' stuff all ower his own yat sneck. Ah spent an hoor trying ti get t' muck off mi hands an' cooat cuffs.

T' owd local bobby used ti ton a blinnd ee ti mooast o' t' goin's on, so long as t' owd fooak an' bairns were left alone. Bud yan year, a new feller, all troosies an' silver buttons' cam inti t' village. He started goin' on aboot hoo it were agin t' law ti let fireworks off i' t' street, an' hoo he wud arrest ivveryan who he caught. Theer's nowt lahk a challenge ti add a bit o' spice ti life. Ah'd estimate there were aboot two hunderd an fifty fireworks let off i' t' main rooad that year, an' he mun hev worn his shoes doon ti his socks wi chessin' t' lads who knew ivvery inch o' that village. He nivver got his arrests, onnyrooad.

T' festivities used ti end aboot arf past nine, wi' rival groups chuckin' ivverythin' they could lay hands on at each ither. And we'd goa hooam, hands an' feeaces bonnt an' mucky, clothes torn, tired, bud very happy.

Ah reckon it'd be called plain vandalism theas days, bud we nivver thowt of it that way — not at t' tahm, onnyrooad!

Michael Park (NR)

Especially funny when it was spoken by the writer himself, this is a satire of a sentimental television advert for Hovis bread. In contemporary South Yorkshire dialect, it is a lasting tribute to Tony Capstick of Mexborough (1944-2003), for thirty years a presenter on Radio Sheffield, and a performer on stage and in television, including The Last of the Summer Wine.

Capstick Comes Home

Ah'll nivver forget that first day at t' pit. Me an' mi fatther worked a seventy-two-hour shift, then wi walked home fo'ty-three mile through t' snow in us bare feet, huddled inside us clothes med out o' old sacks.

Eventually wi trudged ovver t' hill until wi could see t' street light twinklin' in our village. Mi father smiled down at mi through t' icicles hangin' off his nose. 'Nearly home now, lad', he said.

We stumbled into t' house and stood theeare freezin' cold an' tired out, shiverin' an' miserable, in front o' t' meagre fire.

Any road, mi mam says 'Cheer up, lads. Ah've got you some nice brown bread and butter for yer tea.'

Ee, mi fatther went crackers. He reached out and gently pulled mi mam towards 'im bi t' throat. 'Yer big fat, idle ugly wart,' he said. 'You gret useless spawny-eyed parrot-faced wazzock.' ('E had a way wi words, mi fatther. He'd bin to college, y' know.) 'You've been out playin' bingo all afternoon instead o' gettin' some proper snap ready for me an' this lad', he explained to mi poor, little, purple-faced mam.

Then turnin' to me, he said, 'Arthur' (He could never remember mi name) 'here's half a crown. Nip down ter t' chip oyl an' get us a nice piece o' 'addock fer us tea. Man cannot live by bread alone.'

He were a reyt tater, mi father.

He said as 'ow workin' folk should have some dignity an' pride an' self respect, an' as 'ow the' should come home ter summat warm an' cheerful.

An' then he threw mi mam on t' fire.

We didn't 'ave no tellies or shoes or bedclothes. We med us own fun i' them days.

Do you know, when I were a lad you could get a tram down into t' town, buy three new suits an' an ovvercoat, four pair o' good booits, go an' see George Formby at t' Palace Theatre, get blind drunk, 'ave some steak an' chips, bunch o' bananas an' three stone o' monkey nuts — an' still 'ave change out of a farthing.

We'd lots o' things in them days they 'aven't got today — rickets, diptheria, Hitler — and, my, we did look well goin' ter school wi' no backside in us trousers, an' all us little 'eads painted purple because wi 'ad ringworm.

They don't know the're born today!

Tony Capstick (WR)

A homely account in his native East Riding dialect by Brian Spencer, published in the Summer Bulletin *of 1998.*

A Few Wods o' Warnin'

A young fella Ah knaw is gettin wed verra seean, an' Ah feeals really sorry fer 'im. Lass 'e's marryin' worrks at oor spot, an' a reet dainty lartle body she is an' all — nut sahze o' sixpen'orth o copper — an' bonny, bah lad yis! Hooiver, there's a bit of advice Ah'd gie 'im affoor 'e weds orr if Ah could onnly get 'im ti listen. This bit of advice should be telled ti ivvery fella affoor 'e even starts thinkin' o' coourtin'.

When Ah started coourtin' oor lass ... if onnly Ah'd knawn! Ah wor that tekken wi orr that Ah nivver reckoned what a lifetahm o' throuble Ah was bringin' on missen. Ah owt ti ev tummled tiv it a month or twa affoor we get wed. Ah mahnd it as if it wor nobbut yisterda, sha said ti ma this Frida neet: 'Ah'm off ti Brid termorra for a pair o' shoes; yer can come an 'elp me ti choose 'em.'

'Reet, love,' Ah said.

We all 'ad ti worrk Set'da mornins in them daays, o' course, soa, Ah just managed ti get 'oam, get weshed an changed, an' on ti early bus wi'out mi dinner.

'We'll gan in 'ere fosst,' sha says, pushin me intiv a poshleeakin shop i Promenade. 'They're most likely ti ev ma size.'

Noo, to be honest, sahze was summat Ah'd nivver thowt on aboot: colour, shape, price — Ah thowt sha mud teake a bit o' suiting, bud sahze — wha, yer tried a few pair while yer fun' some ti fit! Ooiver, inti shop we gans an sets oorsens doon.

'Pair o' shoes, brown or tan, flat 'eels, lace ups, fer walking in', sha says.

'Certainly madam,' says assistant, 'What size?'

'Two an' aif,' says oor lass.

Bah 'eck, shop lass seeamed ommost gobsthruck at that, an' sha didn't even bother gannin ti seek onny. 'Sorry madam, nothing so small.'

Noo Ah owt ti ev seen danger signal an gi'en orr back wod theer an then, bud Ah wor ower young an' fond, an' Ah suffered for it that daay, bah lad, Ah did an all! We thraipsed fra shop ti shop doon at Quay — Stead an Simpson, Cast an Martin, Benefit, Freeman Hardy's, Co-op — nowt! Bi aboot fower-o-clock we're on bus ti Aud Toon, leeakin at shoe shops i' High Street. An ti think that that deeay was just start o' nigh on fifty year laitin' sahze two an aif shoes!

Then Ah rimember fosst Kessimas present Ah bowt orr efther we wor wed. Ah thowt Ah'd buy orr a new jumper ti gan

wi a new sket sha'd getten. Ah leeaked at label in yan ev orr
frocks ti get right sahze, and then Ah went ti Brid specially ti
buy it wi'oot orr knawin — then Ah just waited for orr ti
oppen parcil o' Kessimas morn. It wor just reet! Colour wer
perfect, reet sahze all ower, onnly sleeaves wor fower inch
ower lang.

'Aye,' sha says. 'Ah've getten verra short arms. That's why
Ah allus knits mi own jumpers.'

That means that whenivver sha buys a coat or a frock,
sleeves esti be shortened. Same wi throosis. Sha gets a pair ti
fit roond waist, an' six inch es ti be lopped off bottom o' slops,
still leaving eneeaf ti tonn up eftherwards. Bah 'ell, Ah reckon
if we could finnd a shop that selled 'em six inch shorter, Ah
bet they'd be a couple o' quid cheaper.

Wah noo, it teeak me a langish tahme ti larn all this, an' Ah
reckon oor lass kept it verra quiet whahle it were ower leate fer
me to do owt aboot it. An — oh aye, Ah've verra nigh fergit-
ten it — that bit ev advice ti young fellas. As Ah said affoore,
it's verra simply really: when it comes to pickin' a lass tha's to
wed, just mek certain, affoore tha starts courtin' orr, that sha
fits inti standard sahze shoes an clothes. Tha'll save thissen a
lifetahm o' throuble an' expense!

Brian Spencer (ER)

*An autobiographical account given by Ernest Beaumont at a
meeting of the Yorkshire Dialect Society, following a visit
underground at Caphouse Colliery, the National Mining
Museum, in October 2000.*

Mi Fust Day dahn t' Pit

Ah fair remember mi fust day dahn t' pit. Ah wor just fo'teen.
Ther' wor plenty o' jobs fer es ter gooa to when wi left t'
schooil, but ther' wo'n't a reight lot o' choice. I' mooast cases
it wor awther t' mill or t' pit. Aye ... t' mill or t' pit — an' ther's
nawther on 'em left nah.

Well ... all mi mates wor off dahn t' pit sooa Ah ed ter gooa
an' all, else the'd 'a' called mi a cissy. Ah didn't know what t'

expect but Ah turned up o' Munda' mornin' afoore six o'clock.

Well ... the' ge' mi a number an' a lamp, sumb'dy turned mi cap back ter frunt, cut a oile in it an' stuck t' lamp in. Fer what good that lamp wor the' mud as well 'a' gin mi a daffodil.

The' said wi wor bahn dahn t' pit in a chair, but it seemed mooare like a lion's cage ter me. Abaht ten on us gor in, an' it went dahn that pit shaft like leetnin. T' pit bottom wor just like a reight big tunnil, but it wor lit up an' whiteweshed. Ther wor little tubs wi wheels on, full uns an' empty uns, all bangin' an' clatterin'. Ah wor a bit flaid, cos ther' wor nooa wheeare ter get aht o' t' rooad.

Ther' wor sooart o' office at one side. The' called it t' box 'oile, an' all t' men wor queuein' up at t' winda ter se what the'r job wor fer that day ... The' daren't tell 'em at pit top, else some on em wunt 'a' gooan dahn ...

Well ... the' telled me ter gooa wi this 'ere collier an' 'e'd show mi ah ter be 'is trammer. Sooa off wi went, shoving one o' theeas empty tubs on t' rails, away inter a tunnil 'at wor baht leets, an' then inter a reight little un afooare the' got ter t' coil face.

T' collier started brayin' at t' coil wi 'is pick, an' when e'd brayed enough dahn an' shovelled it inter t' tub, we set off wi' it inter t' pit bottom. Ah thowt 'Aye, aye, mi trainin's started'. 'E teed 'is motty onter t' tub wi' a bit o' band ('is motty wor a brass disc wi 'is number on sooa the'd know ah much coil ter pay im for when it got ter t' pit top) ...

We took an empty tub back wi us an' when this un wor filled 'e said 'Reight, lad, thar on thi own nah'. Ah thowt 'Aye, aye, mi trainin's finished'. Ah gets mi empty tub like Ah'd bin telled an' sets off back. Oh dear ... Ah wor lost ... an' it wor dark. The' doan't 'ev winda weshers dahn theeare ... an' the' dooan't get sunburnt when the' work baht shirt nawther.

When Ah did get back it wor snap time. Mi mother 'ad put mi some fat an' bread up wi' plenty o' salt on, an' a pop bottle full a cowd watter. By, it wor luvley!

Ah axed t' collier wheeare t' toilet wor ... 'Toilet?' 'e says. 'Ther's nooa toilet dahn 'ere, lad ... tha'll 'ev ter gooa in t' gobbin' ... Ah didn't know what t' gobbin wor nawther, but

Ah fun aht it wor t' space wheeare the'd taen all t' coil thro an' the' threw all t' muck an' rubbish i' theer …

It wor a reight art gooin' ter t' toilet when t' roof wor nobbut two foot 'igh. (An' Ah'll let yer into a little secret … that 'oile wor nivver called a toilet dahn t' pit …)

Well, a few mooare tubs, an' Ah wor fillin 'em an' trammin' 'em an' all, an' it wor 'ooame time … Ah'd addled abaht awf a crahn. Mi mother wod be suited …

Ah came 'ooame an' got batthed in t' tin batth in front o' t' fire. But Ah left a bit o' muck rahnd mi een fer t' other lads ter see … Ah felt like a reight man …

Ernest Beaumont (WR)

Humorous anecdotes

The following are examples of the stories I have heard told, not by stage comedians, but by dialect speakers who know how to make the most of a pithy Yorkshire phrase or punchline. These have been told by such fine raconteurs as Arthur Kinder, Irwin Bielby, Geoff Robinson, Jack Danby, Stanley Ellis and Bill Mitchell.

'Thoo's getten poison i' thi sistren, that's why thoo's bellywark,' says t' docther. 'Thoo mun 'a' thi teeath oot'.

'What?', Ah says. 'All on 'em?'

'Aye', he says. 'ivvery yan'… So Ah took 'em oot, an' laad em on teeable.

A man whose wife had died went to see the monumental mason in his Yorkshire town requesting him to carve on her headstone, 'Lord, she was thine'.

When he visited the graveyard he saw that the inscription read: 'Lord, she was thin'.

Very annoyed, he went back to the mason and said, 'Nay, Ah've come ter play hummer wi thee. Tha's med a reight mullock on it. Tha's gooane an' left t' 'e' off!'

'Oh, dearie me!' said the mason. 'Dooan't thee fret thissen, lad. Ah'll mak it reight fer thi.'

The next time the man saw the gravestone, it read: 'Ee, Lord, she *was* thin.'

An old chap had been seriously ill and went to Scarborough to convalesce. He was doing well, but on the last day of his holiday he collapsed and died. At the funeral they were filing past the open coffin to pay their respects. To please the widow, a friend said to her: 'Ee, 'e looks a lovely colour. That week i' Scarborough must 'a' done 'im good'.

A posh Londoner, driving through the Dales, was not sure of his way, and stopped to ask directions of an old farmer, busy with his cows.

'Now, my man. Can you tell me the way to the abbey?'

'Aye', said the farmer. 'Abaht 'awf a mile up t' rooad tha'll finnd a sign-pooast'.

'Oh, a sign-post, eh? said the Londoner, annoyed not to be given proper directions. 'But suppose I can't read'.

'Well, it'll just suit thi, then,' said the farmer. 'Ther's nowt on it.'

An old lass, a life-long member of the Co-op, had a good turn-up for her funeral. When the minister announced 'We shall now sing hymn number 528', one of her friends turned to her neighbour and said: 'Ee! What a lovely thowt. That wor 'er Co-op number!'

A Yorkshireman arrived at the Pearly Gates. St Peter was astonished. 'Well, Ah nivver!', he said. 'A Yorkshireman! Well, tha can come in, lad. But think on! We'r nut makkin' Yorksher puddin' fer one.'

In a part of the West Riding where they added an extra syllable in words like 'go-ah' and 'so-ah', an inspector went into an RE lesson and said: 'I've a sweet here for the child who can tell me the name of the man who built the ark... Now, boy. Do you know'.

'No-ah!', said the little lad ... But he got the sweet.

In the days before electricity reached the isolated Dales farm-house, an old farmer lay dying, and wanted to have a candle burning by his bed all night. His wife, typically thrifty, felt this would be a waste, and having said good-night to him she was about to take the candle away.

'Nay, lass', he protested. 'Leave it theeare! Ah want t' cannle-leet all thru t' neet'.

'All reight', she said. 'Ah'll leave it. But if tha feels thissen goin' — tha mun blaw it aht!'

The Gospels in dialect

Here are examples of the re-telling of New Testament stories in dialect. First, by Kit Calvert (1903-84), the famed pioneer of cheesemaking in Hawes and uncrowned king of upper Wensleydale. Secondly, by the compiler, from his Ee by Gum, Lord!, *a version of the Gospels in West Riding dialect.*

T' Prodigal Son

Noo, awl t' taxgitherers an' knockaboots crooded roond ta hear Him, an' t' Pharasees an' t' lawyers chuntered an' said, 'This feller tek's up wi' good-fer-nowts an' eyts wi' 'em.'

Sooa, He teld 'em this teeale, an' said: 'Whar's t' man amang ye, if he hed a hunderd sheep, an' lost yan on 'em, 'at wadn't leeave awl t' others on t' fell an' gang an' laate t' strag-gler till he finnds it? An' when he does leet on 't wadn't he lift it ontev his shooders an' hug 't heeame fain an' glad, an' send roond tev his friends an' naybers ta let 'em knaa 'at t' straggler 'd turned up? An' Ah's tellen ye, it's seeame i' heaven. Ther's maar joy ower yah sinner 'at's gitten back, ner ther' is ower ninety-nine 'at yan's nivver had ta laate.

Er what wumman wi' ten bits o' silver, if she was ta loss yan on 'em, wadn't leet a cannel an' ratch ivvery neuk an' coorner till she finnds it? An' when she hez fun 't, she coa's awl t' nay-bers tigither an sez, 'Sharr wi' mi i' mi joy, fer Ah've fun mi silver penny 'at Ah'd lost.' It's just seeame amang t' Angils o' God, if nabbut yar sinner repents.'

Then He said:

'A farmer had tweea lads, an' yan on 'em, t' youngomer, sez teu t' aad feller: "Father, give ez mi sharr ev t' farm, 'at's ta cum ta mi." An seea he let 'em sharr an' sharr alike.

Nut manny days efter, t' youngomer githered awl he'd gitten t'gither, an' teuk hizsel offinta foreign parts, an' thar' weeasted his brass i' lowse leevin'. An' hard times cam' ower t' land he was in, an' he co' ta hey nowt. Seea he went an' hired hizsel, an' his maister sent him inta t' fields ti sarra pigs, an' he'd ha' fain iten t' pig meeat, fer neeabody gev' him owt. Twas than he com' tev his sensis, an' said, "Hoo manny o' mi father's sarvants hez eneugh an' ta spar, an' Ah se fair hungered. Ah'll away heeame ta mi father, an' Ah'll say, 'Father, Ah've sinned agen heaven an' ye, an' Ah's nut fit ta bi coa'd yan o yours. Tak mi on as a sarvant lad'."

Wi' that he gat up an' set off heeame, an' his father spied him cummen' when he was a lang way off, an' he was wheea fer him, an' ran oot ta meet him, an' threw his arms roond his neck an' kissed him, fer he was fain ta see him. An' t' lad said, "Father, Ah've sinned agen heaven an' dun a gert wrang t' ye an' Ah's nut fit t' bi coa'd a lad ev yours."

But t' father coa'd sarvants, tellen' 'em ta hurry up an' fetch t' best suit o' cleeas th' cud finnd, an' help him t' don, an' git a ring fer his finger, an' shun fer his feet, an' fetch t' fattest cauf in, an' kill't — "Sooa ez we may awl it an' bi joyful, Fer mi lad 'at Ah thowt was deead 's alive. We had him lost, but noo he's fun ageean." An' th' started ta enjoy th'sels.

Noo t' owder lad was oot in t' fields an' as he co' near t' hoose he heeard music an' dancin'. An' coa'en yan ev t' sarvants aside he ast what wez on, an' t' sarvant teld him, "Thi bruther's cum'd heeame, an' becos he's back seeafe an' soond thi father's kill't t' fat cauf."

He then went crazy, an' wadn't gang in. Seea his father cam' oot t' tice him, but he pleeaned tev his father, "Awl t' years o' mi life hev Ah bin like a sarvant, dun awl thoo ast er teld mi, an' yet nivver ez mich ez a lile gooat hez t' gin mi, seea's Ah cud hev a merry neet wi' mi mates. But as seun as this weeastrel co's back, efter squanderen awl thoo gev' him i' lowse livin' an' fancy wimmin, thoo kills t' best stalled cauf fer him."

But t' father says tew him; "Mi lad! Thoo's awlis wi' mi, an' awl Ah hev is thine. It's nobbut reet yan sud mak' merry an' bi joyful; fer thi bruther 'at we thowt was deead's alive. He was lost, an' noo he's fun".'

Kit Calvert (NR)

T' Prodigal Lad

Nah it wor some varry stuck-up fowk knawn as Pharisees 'at un knowin'ly got Jesus ter tell one of 'is mooast famous tales. Tha sees, they'd been chunterin' an' carryin' on because Jesus wor spendin' a lot of 'is time talkin' ter tax-gatherers an' such-like — fowk 'at t' Pharisees thowt as common as muck. An' one day Jesus turns ter t' Pharisees, an' 'e says ...

The' wor once a well-ter-do farmer 'at 'ad two lads. T' youngest on 'em comes up to 'is fatther, an' 'e says: 'Fatther, will ta gi'e me my share o' t' land?' T' farmer must a' been reight ta'en aback bi this. T' deeacent thing ter do is ter cahr quiet till thi fatther dees afooare tha starts axin' fer thi legacy. 'Ahivver, t' fatther thowt 'e'd gi'e t' lad a chance — see what 'e could do on 'is awn, like — so 'e gev 'im 'is share o' t' land.

Well, would yer credit it? No sooiner does 'e gerr 'is 'ands on it than t' lad sells it all, taks all t' brass, an' goes off inter foreign parts. An' theeare 'e 'as a grand owd time, blewin' in all 'is brass, wi' all 'is mates, an' plenty o' fancy-women. 'E stays up till all 'ahrs, an' mooast o' t' time 'e's as drunk as a wheeal-'eead.

Ah, but when 'e'd spent all 'is brass, it wor a different tale! 'E'd no mates then, ner lady-friends nawther. An' 'e ended up wi' a bit of a job on a farm, lookin' after t' pigs. By Gum! What a come-dahn fer a Jeew! The' think ther's nowt muckier ner a pig, tha knaws, does t' Jeews. But even though it sickened 'im off — 'e 'ad ter do it. Ee! an' 'e wor that 'ungry 'e could've getten dahn on 'is 'ands an' knees an' etten t' pig-swill!

Then, all of a sudden, t' lad comes to 'is senses. 'Ee, Ah am a fooil!' 'e says to 'issen. 'A reight blether-'eead! Ther's fowk workin' fer mi fatther 'at can eyt an' sup ter the'r 'eart's content. An' 'ere am I, pinin' ter deeath! Ah mun go back to mi fatther. Ah s'll say to 'im: "Fatther, Ah've done wrong. Ah'm nooan fit to be a son o' thine. Gi'e us a job as one o' thi farmworkers." That's all Ah ax.'

So 'e sets off back 'ooam, an' after trailin' monny a mile 'e lands up i' regs an' tatters, an' wi' an empty belly. But a long while afooare 'e gets ter t' farm 'is fatther sees 'im, an' instead o' goin' off at t' deep end, 'e rushes aht to meet 'im, thraws 'is arms rahn t' lad, an' kisses 'im — 'E felt that sorry fer 'im, tha sees.

T' poor lad starts t' speech 'at 'e'd re'earsed: 'Fatther, Ah've done wrong. Ah'm nooan fit to be a son o' thine —'. But 'is fatther butts in, an' calls aht ter t' servants:

'Come on! Frame yersens! This lad's starvin' aht 'ere — frozzen ter deeath! Bring 'im summat wahrm ter weear — bring 'im mi top coit ... An' 'e's nowt on 'is feet. Bring 'im a pair o' booits ... An' go an' kill yon cawf i' t' mistal — t' one 'at we've been fettenin' up. We're bahn to 'ave a celebration ... Ah thowt this lad o' mine wor deead — an' 'e's alive ageean! Ah thowt 'e wor lost — an' 'e's come back 'ooam!'

An' sooin the' wer 'evin' a proper 'ooam-comin', wi' food, an' mewsic, an' lively dancin'. It wor a reight gooid do, Ah'll tell thi!

But t' lad's elder brutther wor still workin' aht i' t' fields. At t' end o' t' day, when 'e got near t' 'ahse, 'e 'eeard mewsic an' dancin'. 'E says ter t' servants: 'What's up? What's all t' celebrations abaht?'

'It's thi' brutther!' they answer. ''E's come back 'ooam, an' thi fatther's as pleased as Punch, cos 'e's nut come to onny 'arm.'

But t' elder brutther wor fewrious. An' 'e stood theeare i' t' yard, sulkin' away, an' refewsin' ter go in. In a bit, 'is fatther come aht to 'im, an' started pleadin' wi' 'im to come in, an' stop bein' such a jealous mawk.

'Nay, fatther', says t' lad. 'Ah've slaved fer thee all these years. Ah've worked mi' fingers ter t' booane, an' Ah've nivver done owt to upset thi. But tha's nut gi'en me even so much as a bit o' gooat meyt, so Ah could thraw a party fer mi' mates. But as sooin as this son o' thine turns up, after chuckin' all that brass dahn t' drain, an' livin' wi' fancy-women — tha' goes an' kills t' fetted cawf fer 'im!'

'Nay, lad', says t' fatther. 'Tha's allus been one o' t' family — an' tha can 'ave owt tha wants — but terday's summat special. Wi couldn't but mak a bit of a fuss. Wi thowt this brutther o' thine wor deead — an' 'e's alive ageean. Wi thowt e' wor lost — an' 'e's come back 'ooam.'

Well, that's wheeare t' stooary ends — but Ah bet it gev yon Pharisees summat ter think abaht — 'cos the' wer' just like t' elder brutther, tha knaws — allus takkin' a pride i' the'r achievements. An' when Jesus said 'at t' Almighty — like this fatther — could fergive 'is childer, so long as they awned up the'd done wrong — the' didn't like it one bit. The' wer' funny-ossities wer' t' Pharisees — An' Ah reckon ther's plenty on 'em abaht terday, an' all. Nay, y'd 'a' thowt yon lad 'ould 'a' been glad ter see 'is brutther — t' self-reighteous monkey! Eh dear! Ther's nowt so queer as fowk.

Arnold Kellett (WR)

T' Nativity

Noo it cam aboot i them days 'at Caesar Agustus gav oot an order 'at aw t' fooak 'at leeaved i t' countries 'at he was maister on, had to bi coonted, an' this coontin was deun at t' time Quirinas was t' Guvener i Syria. An' ivvery body had te gang ez weel te ther aan toon te bi coonted. An' Joseph had te gang ez weel fra Nazareth i' Galilee te Bethlehem, David's toon i' Judea, fer he was yan ev David's breed, an' thar bi coonted wi Mary his wife et was at t' time expecten.

An' seea it happened 'at while thu war thar, t' time co' roond 'at t' babby sud bi booarn, an' 'twas a lad, her first, an' she lapped him in a barrie coaat an' laid him in a manger, fer ther was neea room fer 'em i' t' ludgin' hoose.

An, ther was i t' seeam countryside shipperds oot i' t' fields leuken efter ther yowes owerneet. An' an angil ev t' Lord's co tew 'em, an' t' glory ev t' Lord shone aw roond 'em, an' thu war turribly freetened. An' t' angil said, 'Dooat bi freetened, fer ther's nowt te bi freetened on, fer Ah's fetchen ye good news ev gert joy fer aw t' world. Fer ther's bin booarn te-day i' David's toon, a Saviour, Christ the Lord. An' te prove to ye 'at it is seea, ye'll finnd t' babby lapped i' a barrie cooat an' liggen in a manger.

An' aw at yance ther was wi that angil a heeal crood ev t' seeam heavenly fooak praisen God an' singen, 'Glory te God i' t' heighest heaven an' on earth peeace an' goodwill te men.'

An' when t' angils had geean back te heaven, t' shipperds said yan tev another, 'Let's away te Bethlehem and see fer wersels what t' Lord meead knaan tew ez'. An' away the went as fast as the cu, an the fan Mary an' Joseph an t' babby liggen in a manger.

An' efter the'd sin Him, the telt ivverybody aw 'at the'd bin telt aboot Him bi t' Angil choir. An' aw 'at heeared aboot it was fair mazed at t' teeals 'at was telt em bi t' shipperds.

But Mary, his Mother, said nowt aboot these things tev annibody, but manny a time she pondered ower em in her thowts. An' t' shipperds went back to ther wark, but glorfyen God fer aw the'd heeard an' seen beeath oot i' fields an' i' t' steeable.

Kit Calvert (NR)

T' Babby Born in a Mistal

Nah ther' wor a two-a-thri shepherds 'oo t' same neet 'appened ter bi aht i' t' fields near Bethle'em, sitting rahnd the'r campfire, keepin' watch ovver the'r sheep.

All of a sudden, says Sent Lewk, these 'ere shepherds see t' sky breeten up wi' a gloorious blaze o' leet 'at shines all rahnd 'em. Well, the'r flaid ter deeath! An' while the're cahrin' theeare on t' grahnd, as weak as watter, an' all of a dither, t' Angil o' t' Lord says tul 'em:

'Nay, there's nowt ter bi afeeared on. Ah've come ter bring

thi some reight cheerful neews — neews 'at 'll gladden all t' fowk 'oo 'ear it. Ther's a little lad just been born i' Bethle'em — t' royal city o' David, tha knaws. An' this little lad is t' Messiah, t' Saviour of all mankind. An' does-ta knaw wheeare tha'll finnd t' babby? Tha'll finnd 'im in a mistal, liggin' in a manger, all wahrm an' cooasy in 'is 'ippins.'

No sooiner 'as t' Angil finished 'is message than t' shepherds 'ear wonderful singin' 'at fills all t' sky — a sooart of Allelewia Chooarus sung bi thahsands an' thahsands of angil voices.

'Glooary ter God', the' sing. 'Glooary in t' 'ighest 'eaven. An' peace on earth, an' gooidwill sent dahn from 'eaven ter men!'

But this 'ere 'eavenly visitation wor a bit ovver-pahrin' fer t' shepherds. As Ah've said, at fust the' wer' flaid ter deeath. An' when it wor all ovver, the' wer' that capped the' just gawped at one another. Then one on 'em says:

'Na then, lads, wi mun go an' see if t' tale 'at t' angil 'as telled us is reight. Wi mun go inter Bethle'em an' try to finnd this 'ere babby.'

'But what abaht t' sheep?', says another on 'em.

'Oh, 'ummer ter t' sheep!' says t' fust shepherd.' This is summat aht o' t' ordinary — it's a message from t' Almighty! T' sheep 'll nut come to onny 'arm. It's nobbut a mile away. Come on, lad. Frame thissen!'

So off the' go, an' by an' by the' finnd this little mistal, an' Mary and Joseph, an' t' babby liggin' in a manger.

'Can wi 'ave a peep at 'im?' axed one o' t' shepherds.

'Aye, tha can that', says Joseph, glad of a bit o' company, like.

'Ee! I'n't 'e grand?' says t' shepherd. 'E's that bonny an' tender, 'e's same as a neew-born lamb ... What do the' call thi, then, little feller?'

'We'r bahn to call 'im Jesus,' says Mary. 'Nah, if tha'll excuse mi, it's time fer 'is next feed.'

So Mary sam's t' bairn up aht o' t' manger, an' sits 'ersen dahn ter feed 'im. An' off t'shepherds go, thrilled ter bits 'at the've seen t' little Lord Jesus.

Well, later on Mary and Joseph 'ave a visit from a different sooart o' fowk altogether — Wise Men bringin' the'r precious gifts o' gowd, frankincense an' myrrh. Tha can read abaht that i' Sent Mattheew's Gospil. An' then ther's Sent John 'at tells us 'at, when Jesus wor born, it wor nowt less ner God Almighty becomin' flesh an' blood, an' dwellin' among us. But what appeals ter me, tha knaws, is this simple, 'omely tale telled bi Sent Lewk. It's same as if 'e's sayin' 'at t' Lord really cares abaht ordinary fowk — same as yon shepherds — an' fowk wi' no brass, an' none o' t' comforts an' luxuries wi tak fer granted. It's summat we oft ferget at Christmastime.

Arnold Kellett (WR)

Further reading

Yorkshire Lyrics (1898), John Hartley
The English Dialect Dictionary (1905), Joseph Wright
Yorkshire Wit, Character etc (1911), R Blakeborough
Goodies (1912, 1990), W F Turner
Yorkshire Dialect Poems (1916), ed F W Moorman
Songs of the Ridings (1918), F W Moorman
Yorkshire Dialect Prose (1944, 1945), ed W J Halliday, B Dickens
The White Rose Garland (1949), ed W J Halliday, S Umpleby
Yorkshire Lyrics (1960), D A Ratcliffe
A Cleveland Anthology (1963), ed Bill Cowley
West Riding Dialect Verse (1964), ed Gwen Wade
Dialect Verse from the Ridings (1970), ed Bill Cowley *et al*
Yorkshire Dialect (1970), J Waddington-Feather
Emily Brontë and Haworth Dialect (1970), K M Petyt
A Bonny Hubbleshoe (1970), Margaret Batty
The Muse went Weaving (nd), Fred Brown
The Yorkshire Pudding Almanack (1974), ed Dyson & Ellis
Lang Sarmons (1974, 1992), Arthur Jarratt
The Yorkshire Yammer (1975), Peter Wright
Poems from the Yorkshire Dales (1979), Gordon Jefferson
East Yorkshire Miscellany (1981), Jack Danby
Pennine Thowts (1982, 1991), Doris Beer
Words Through T' Shuttle Ee (1983), ed Gerald England
A Levelheeaded Dalesbred Lass (1988), Ruth Dent
East Yorkshire Facts and Fables (1989), ed Norman Stockton
Cum thi Ways In (1990), Ruth Dent
Kirkbridge Kaleidoscope (1991), Michael Park
Scriptural Readings in Yorkshire Dialect (1991), ed T M Cluderay
Basic Broad Yorkshire (1992), Arnold Kellett
Ee by Gum, Lord! (1996), Arnold Kellett
Goin' tu t' Spaws (1996), ed Muriel Shackleton

A Century of Yorkshire Dialect (1997), ed Dewhirst & Kellett
Yorkshire Words Today (1997), ed Paynter, Upton, Widdowson
On Ilkla Mooar Baht 'At (1998), Arnold Kellett
One for t' Rooad (1999), Don Halliday
How they Lived in the Yorkshire Dales (2001), W R Mitchell
Songs of the Ridings (2001), collected by M & N Hudleston
The Yorkshire Dictionary of Dialect, Tradition and Folklore
    (2002, revised edition), Arnold Kellett

Other publications featuring dialect material include
Transactions and *Summer Bulletin* each published annually by
the Yorkshire Dialect Society, and the *Dalesman* magazine, in
particular Arnold Kellett's series 'Yorkshire Words' (1994-9)
and 'Yorkshire Speyks' (2000-2), illustrated by Margaret
Clarkson.
    Audio cassettes available from the YDS: *First o' t' Sooart*
(Ilkley Festival), *Ee By Gum Lord!* (Arnold Kellett) and *West
Riding Tales* (Arthur Kinder).

Useful addresses:
    Michael Park, secretary, Yorkshire Dialect Society,
51 Stepney Avenue, Scarborough, North Yorkshire YO12 5BW.
    Doreen Putnam, secretary, East Riding Dialect Society,
19 Welton Old Road, Welton, East Yorkshire HU15 1NV.

Glossary

This includes words not easily guessed from the context, but not the many which are simply spelt differently in order to show the dialect pronunciation, such as words like *cann'le* (candle), *sooin* or *seean* (soon) and *theeare* (there). Note that *ah* (WR) and *oo* (NER) replace normal English *ou* in words like *rahnd* and *roond* (round). For further information, including derivations, see the *Yorkshire Dictionary of Dialect, Tradition and Folklore* and the *English Dialect Dictionary*.

aboon above
addle to earn
afooare before
agaan, ageean again; against, opposite
agate busy with
ammot am not
anent next to
'arston, 'earthstun hearthstone
'assnook space below fire-grate
aud, awd old
'avverbreead oat-bread
awther either

back-end autumn
bahde, bard to stay; bear
bahn going
baht without
bairn, barn child
band string (*in t' nick*), friendship etc kept ticking over
belly-wark stomach-ache
besom broom
birks birches
blether bladder
bogie go-kart
bo'n to burn

brant steep
brasst burst
brat apron, smock
bray to hit
breead-fleg ceiling-rack
brussen-guts glutton
bullace wild plum
bum-baillie bailiff, rent man
cadger shop cheap general store
cahr to stay, squat
canty cheerful
cap to surprise; beat, surpass
cham'er bedroom
champion excellent
chapil-lowsin' coming out after the end of a service
cheg to chew
cheany earthenware
checker brat woolsorter's apron
chewse'ah no matter how
childer children
chunter to grumble, mutter
cinder tay cinder tea (for soothing babies)
claht cloth; to hit
clais clothes

clart   to daub
cleg   horse-fly
closit   outdoor lavatory
cock-leet   dawn
creeaked   crooked
curn   currant

despert   extremely
ding   to throw violently
doff   to take off
dooaf   dough
doorstun   doorstep
dowly   poorly, in low spirits
doy   dear, darling
dree   dreary, wearisome
druffen   drunk

'eart-sluffened   very upset
ee!   expression of
   surprise or annoyance
een   eyes

fahl   ugly
fain   glad
fang   to take
fend   to manage
feat   lively
fet   fit, sufficient
fettle   to clean, tidy
fick   to struggle
firepoint   poker
flayed, flaid, fleered   frightened
flaysome   terrifying
fleet   glowing embers
fooadyard   farmyard
fooarced, fooast   forced; certain
   (to)
forthy   therefore
foss   waterfall
frame thissen   get organised
fratch   (to) quarrel
frid   from the
frummerty   spiced, wheaten
   Christmas porridge
fun   found

fuzzock   donkey
gaat, gait   gate, way
gain   near
gallusses   braces, straps
gan, gang   to go, walk
gaum   notice, sense
gawp   to stare
gay   to go
gimmer   ewe before it lambs
ginnel   narrow passage
   between buildings
gip   to want to vomit
gliff   glance
Gow, Gum   euphemisms for
   God
gradely   excellent (mostly
   Lancs)

haile   well
happins   bedclothes
hawf   half
heft   handle (of tool)
hime   hoar frost
hoaf   half
hosen   stockings
hubbleshoo   confusion, jumble
hug   to carry
hummer   euphemism for hell

immer threng   housework
'ippins   nappies, swaddling-
   clothes
ivver   ever

jannock   fair, right
jock   food

kall   to chat, gossip
kelterment   odds and ends
ken   to make known
kittle   delicately balanced
knap   to crunch
kye   cattle

laat, lait, late   to look for

laik   to play
lair, laith(e)   barn
lap   to wrap
lawn   fine-quality cloth
lay, ley   scythe
layky   playful
leet-gi'en   flirtatious
lig   to lie
loiner   person living in a lane
lop   flea
lownd   calm
lowp   to leap
lowse   to finish, close
lug   ear
lyke   corpse

marrer   somebody exactly like
   somebody else
mawk   maggot; surly person
mawngy   surly, uncooperative
mell   to meddle
mennies   minnows
mense   decency; common sense
mickle   much
mistal   cow-shed
moggy   parkin
moil   drudgery
moock middin   rubbish heap
mowdiwarp   mole
mud   might
mullock   mess
mun   must

nawther   neither
neean, nooan   not; none
neive   fist
nengin'   nagging
ner   than
nessy   outside toilet
nim   light and brisk
nithered   feeling very cold
nobbut   only
nobby   posh
noo-cauven   newly calved
nowt   nothing

nu'ss   nurse
oard   old
'od   to hold
'odder   holder
'oile   hole, place
ooin   to harass, upset
'oss   horse
'ossin ter slaht   coming on to
   rain
Owd Lad   the Devil
owerend   standing up
owt   anything
parzel   to move cautiously
pattens   clogs with irons on
   sole
pawse   to kick
peff   slight cough
perfyte   perfect
pestil   leg of pork
phiz   face
piggin   can with handle
pinfowd   pound (for strays)
pissimer   ant
pleeaf, ploghe   plough
plother   to wade
pooak   bag
possnit   small pan
posser   copper-headed washday instrument
possit   hot, milky drink

rammle   to stuff in
ratchin'   hedgehog
ratten   rat
recklin   weakest of the litter
rew   to regret
rigg   back
rive   to tear
rooar   to cry
rowels   spurs

sackless   ineffectual, lacking in
   effort
saig   to saw
sair   sore

sam to pick (up)
sarra to feed
sawl soul
seer sure
seeat soot
set pot fixed boiler
sewer sure
shakked i' bits crazy
shoe-soil shoe sole
shoon shoes
side to put away, tidy
sike such
sind to rinse
sistren system
sither! Look!
skrike to screech
slaap slippery
slaht to splash
slyke such
smittle to infect
snizy bitingly cold and damp
snod smooth
sooalin' huge
snap packed lunch
spice cake (Christmas) cake
stalled fed up (with), tired of
starne star
starved feeling very cold
starved-un person who easily feels cold
stee ladder
steeanchecker stonebreaker
stiddy anvil
sud should
swound unconsciousness
taws marbles
tee to tie
tentin' watching over
tew to toil, struggle
theeak to thatch

thible stick for stirring
thick seeam kind of tripe
thimmle thimble
thiseln, thissen yourself
thrang, throng busy; crowded
thruff through
tiv, tul, tuv to
to-morn tomorrow
to'n to turn
trig to fill
twisters and turners workers in textile mills
tyke dog; Yorkshireman

vast o' a lot of
voider wicker clothes basket

wahr worse; war
wame stomach
wankly weak
wark ache; work
wazzock fool
wengby old and hard cheese
wheel-'eead hub
whinnies gorse, furze
whisht silent
wick life; week
willent won't
winder to winnow; window
winter-'edge clothes horse

yah, yan, yar one
yam home
yance once
yark to pull with a jerk
yat-stowp gate-post
yeroil ear-hole
yond that (person)
Yorkshire bite a cunning dealer

Other dialect titles available from Dalesman

Yorkshire Dictionary of Dialect, Tradition and Folklore
Arnold Kellett

More than 3,000 entries span work and domestic life, lore and legend, sport and recreation, and natural features.

'... a comprehensive "bible" of the Broad Acres.' *Evening Post*

£8.95 pbk
1 85825 016 1

Ee By Gum, Lord!
Arnold Kellett

The Gospels as retold by a Tyke. What better way to understand Jesus's message than through the down-to-earth language of ordinary folk?

'...you can feel the power in the text.' *Salvation Army Living Waters*

£6.95 pbk
1 85825 065 x

A catalogue of all Dalesman magazines, books, calendars and videos/DVDs can be obtained from

Country Publications Ltd, The Water Mill, Broughton Hall, Skipton, North Yorkshire BD23 3AG, UK

Tel: (+44) 01756 701033
Email: sales@dalesman.co.uk
Website: www.dalesman.co.uk